the

sex

book

A no-nonsense guide for teenagers

Jane Pavanel

Published in the U.K. in 2003 by Wizard Books, an imprint of Icon Books Ltd., Grange Road, Duxford, Cambridge CB2 4QF.
Tel. 01763 208 008
Fax. 01763 208 080
e-mail: wizardbooks@iconbooks.co.uk
www.iconbooks.co.uk/wizard

Sold in the U.K. and Eire by Faber and Faber Ltd., 3 Queen Square, London WCIN 3AU, or their agents.
Originally published in the U.S.A. and Canada in 2001 by Lobster Press™, 1620 Sherbrooke Street West, Suites C&D,
Montréal, Québec H3H 1C9, Canada.
www.lobsterpress.com

Publisher of US-Canadian edition: Alison Fripp
Editor of US-Canadian edition: Kim Bourgeois
Illustrations: Grant Cunningham
Book design: Antoinette Morielli

ISBN 1 84046 472 0

Text copyright © 2001 Jane Pavanel
Illustrations copyright © 2001 Lobster Press™

The author has asserted her moral rights.

Typesetting by Wayzgoose

Printed and bound in Singapore by Tien Wah Press

To Sam,
My best friend, lover, and husband

ACKNOWLEDGEMENTS

I have always loved people who are open, frank, intelligent, generous, and caring. Their interest in life and their willingness to engage with others make them very easy to be with. Meeting people who fit this description is a rare event, though not so rare, I discovered, when I began to seek advice from that segment of the population that works with teenagers every day. There I encountered many women and men with the qualities listed above and was lucky to have the help of several of them in the researching and writing of this book. They shared their knowledge, experience, and wisdom freely, and while doing so, were a daily inspiration. For all of this, and for going over the manuscript so carefully, I thank Sue Mckenzie, Dr. Pierre Tellier, Sholem Krishtalka, Karen Mendell, and Martine Drapeau. The manuscript also benefited from the thoughtful reading of Leah Schwantz, who frequently put me back on track. Other readers who provided valuable insights and timely support were Adam Schwantz, Cynthia Scotland, Ada Sinacore, Sara Morley, Annie and François Murphy, and my friend Lynn Horton, who would have done more if circumstances had permitted. Alison Fischer, Jennifer Zakutney, and Angie Dimitriou not only read and commented on the manuscript, but were unstinting in their roles as research assistants. Thank you so much for your help.

I am also very grateful to have the friendship of Louise Jarrett, a devoted high school teacher whose abiding regard for her students was part of the genesis of this book. Candice Higgs, another teacher of energy and enthusiasm, was instrumental in giving me access to the questions, concerns, and ideas of teenagers on the subject of sex. To the teens themselves, students at Trinity College School in Ontario who boldly answered my questionnaire, a heartfelt thank you and best wishes for the future.

Other people I want to acknowledge who offered expertise and good vibrations are Barbara Victor, Pat Caldwell, Tom Fowler, Betty Goldwarg, Anne-Marie Martinez, Jim Washer, David Pavanel, Emily Cummins, Andrew Arcand, my friend Merry Ellen Scully Mosna, and my sisters Dr. Ellen Schwantz and Alex Froome, the latter of whom shared personal experiences that helped me clarify what I wanted to communicate about sex. I was also fortunate to have the excellent guidance of Kim Bourgeois, my editor, a woman of great patience and diplomacy. Her caring attention to meaning and details of every kind made this a much better book. Of course, there would be no book without the unwavering support of my publisher, Alison Fripp, who offered me the kind of interest and commitment that most writers can only dream of. For that, I feel lasting affection and gratitude.

Many times as I sat in front of my computer I knew what I wanted to say, but didn't know how to say it. At such moments all I had to do was think of my children, Hannah, May, and Jack, and of their keen and natural desire to receive information that would help them make decisions about their lives. For constantly reminding me of the importance of knowing what and why, I thank them every day of my life.

Other family members I wish to thank for their love and positive influence are my brother John and sister Joanne, my dad Charlie Pavanel and his new wife Vivian, and my very dear Aunt Joan. Finally, for his sound judgement and unending support, I owe a special thanks to Sami Antaki, my husband.

For this U.K. edition of the book, I would like to thank Dr. Chris Sonnex of Addenbrookes Hospital, Cambridge, who kindly read the text in order to bring it in line with U.K. practice; Margaret McGovern at the Family Planning Association, who was instrumental in sourcing many of the facts applicable to the U.K.; and Jennifer Rigby of Wizard Books, who managed the whole project, editing the book with great care and attention. This edition would not have appeared without their unfailing support.

Jane Pavanel

INTRODUCTION

Sex is a big, big part of life. It's exciting, confusing, liberating, and mysterious…and you probably wonder how you're ever going to figure it out. The thing is, you don't suddenly figure out sex, you learn about it at your own pace, pretty much as you're learning about yourself and the world around you. Over time, you'll find out what you like and don't like, what's right for you and what isn't.

There are endless ways to feel desire, think about love, and respond to the sensations of touching someone and being touched. Your experiences will be entirely your own, and the decisions you make about what to do next will be personal too. But as you're making those decisions, it will help if you know as much as you can about the human body, how sex works, the consequences of sexual activities, and your own feelings, ideas, values, and expectations.

This book offers 198 pages of helpful information, including insights into why girls and guys behave the way they do, questions and answers about sex, facts about what's true and what isn't, and valuable resources. To make it easy to find what you want, everything is presented in an A to Z format. But you don't have to read it in that order. Read it any way you like at any time of day or night, and take pleasure in feeling more confident about sex. The more you learn, the better decisions you'll make about your body.

Sex Symbols

 Speaks DIRECTLY to female readers

 Speaks DIRECTLY to male readers

 Takes a closer look at the facts

 Answers your questions

Aaah

It can take years to feel comfortable with sex or it can happen right away. However it is for you, learning about sex and how to express yourself as a sexual being is an amazing and interesting journey, sometimes a lot of fun, sometimes confusing or painful. Then one day, after the climax, you experience "aaah." Now you're getting somewhere. This is the shining moment when you feel happy with your partner and with yourself and the sex is great. "Aaah" is about satisfaction and pleasure and feeling right about what you're doing and who you're doing it with, whatever your age, whatever your sexual orientation.

♂

Guys are usually hit by strong emotions when they hear their girlfriend or someone they had sex with is pregnant. They may feel many things, including confusion, guilt, anger, fear, or sadness. Some guys are proud and happy. Whatever your feelings, if this happens to you, it's good if you can express them in an open way with your partner. She can support you by listening, and you can support her by caring about her well-being and respecting her decision. If she wants to have an abortion, you can help plan and pay for it (if necessary), and you can accompany her when it's being done. You may not agree with abortion, but by law you can't force anyone to have a baby.

Abortion ♀

Having an abortion means ending your pregnancy. It involves getting a doctor to remove the developing embryo from your uterus as soon as possible once you discover you're pregnant. When you ask a doctor to end your pregnancy for personal reasons, it's called an elective abortion. A therapeutic abortion is performed when a doctor thinks the pregnancy places your health at risk. A spontaneous abortion, or miscarriage, is when the embryo aborts itself, whether or not you want to have the baby.

If you decide to have an abortion, it's very important to have it early, before the embryo is 12 weeks old. That way it's much, much safer, and it's almost always quicker, less painful, and, if you are paying at a private clinic, less expensive. One thing you should never do is try to give yourself an abortion. It won't work, and worse, you could hurt yourself badly or even die. For a safe abortion, see a doctor. See Abortion Pill, Birth Control, Embryo, Emergency Contraception, Foetus.

First 12 weeks

The most common way to perform an abortion during the first 12 weeks of pregnancy (also called the first trimester) is by vacuum suction. A doctor puts a small tube into your vagina, through your cervix, and gently vacuums out the contents of your uterus. This is performed under a light general anaesthetic, or sometimes with a local anaesthetic. For some women this feels painful; others only feel a bit of discomfort. The actual operation takes only a few minutes and is very safe. It's normal to have bleeding and cramping after the abortion, possibly for several days. Staff at the clinic or hospital will tell you how to deal with it. But if you find you're bleeding more than during your period, call a doctor. On rare occasions vacuum suction can lead to serious problems.

Abortion

From 12 to 24 weeks

It's more complicated to have an abortion between 12 and 24 weeks (also called the second trimester). The foetus is more developed and therefore requires larger instruments to be removed from the uterus. The uterus is also softer at this stage, which means it can be damaged more easily. And since your pregnancy is further along, you may have more intense feelings about the life that's growing inside you. But if you feel certain you want to end your pregnancy, there are still several ways of aborting the foetus. All of them have risks attached, though it's no riskier to have an abortion at this stage than it is to give birth. The method decided on will depend on the doctor's training, the equipment available, and the approaches used in your area.

Some doctors perform a termination by vacuum suction between 12 and 14 weeks. But it's unusual to perform this after 14 weeks.

Availability

Elective abortions are legal in England, Scotland and Wales, but illegal in Northern Ireland. Even in Great Britain, some doctors refuse to perform them. However, many women choose to attend a private clinic where they can pay to have their pregnancy terminated. Waiting lists for NHS abortions vary in different parts of the country, but if you are considering terminating a pregnancy you are best off first seeing your G.P. or attending a family planning clinic, or telephoning a sexual health clinic or pregnancy help line for advice. There are also many web sites that offer reliable information on abortion and choice. See the Resources section at the back of this book for further info.

Support ♀

If you discover you're pregnant, you'll probably find it a big help to talk about your feelings and options. It's great if you can discuss these things with your boyfriend. It's also good if you can confide in a trusted friend or parent. Breaking the news to family is always tough, but after the initial shock or disappointment, there's a good chance your parents will stand behind your decision. Even if the guy involved is not your boyfriend, he should know what's going on. Telling him about the pregnancy gives him the chance to be responsible. If you decide to abort, hopefully he'll be helpful by offering comfort, information, and financial support if necessary.

Every year in the U.K. about 40,000 teenagers have an abortion.

Emotions ♀

Deciding whether or not to continue a pregnancy is a big responsibility. If you're faced with this decision, it's normal to feel many emotions at once, such as anxiety, amazement, uncertainty, determination, fear, sadness, anger, or guilt. Many girls who discover they're pregnant examine their situation and know immediately that they want to have an abortion. Afterwards, they continue to feel right about their decision, as well as . . .

Parental consent

Parental consent is not required no matter what your age. However, the doctor seeing you will need to ensure that you are mature enough to understand what is proposed and understand the nature and possible consequences of having a termination.

Making the decision

Because a pregnancy that's carried to term usually produces a healthy child, many people have strong feelings about abortion. Some people are against it because they believe the embryo is a tiny human being that has the right to life. They refer to themselves as pro-life. Others argue that each woman has the right to make her own decisions about her body and future. These people refer to themselves as pro-choice. What are your thoughts and feelings about abortion? If one day you find out you're pregnant, knowing your position will help you decide how to go forward.

Abortion Pill ♀
↘RU-486 mifepristone

There's another common way to end a pregnancy, that involves taking a pill called called RU-486 (mifepristone) followed by a second pill, usually misoprostol, inserted into the vagina 2 days later.

RU-486 is actually a code name for the drug mifepristone. The effect of this drug when taken in the first 9 weeks of pregnancy is to break down the lining of the uterus. The embryo, which is nestled in the lining, is dislodged. The second pill makes the uterus contract. Over the next several hours these contractions push the uterine lining out of the body, along with the

Abortion Pill

embryo, in a flow of heavy bleeding. Light bleeding may continue for 2 to 3 weeks. It is essential to take the second pill otherwise a termination may not be successful; if the foetus survives, it could potentially be harmed by the first pill.

Both pills must be taken under nurse or doctor supervision. A third visit to the doctor is necessary to make sure the abortion worked and that everything is okay. Taking these pills is considered to be very safe and is 95% effective in ending pregnancies.

Advantages

Many doctors who won't perform surgical abortions are comfortable offering these pills, making abortion more widely available. Women can abort as soon as they know they're pregnant (for a surgical abortion, they must wait at least 6 weeks from the time of conception). There are none of the risks associated with surgery, such as infection or damage to the uterus or cervix. Cramping and bleeding are minimal and no more severe than following early surgical abortion. Women aborting this way have more control and privacy.

Disadvantages

Only works during the first weeks of pregnancy. With 2 trips to the doctor's office over 3 days, it's a "long" abortion. Side effects of misoprostol include mild nausea, vomiting, cramping, and diarrhea (these side effects usually disappear within a few days). Excessive bleeding occurs in rare cases. For medical reasons, not all women are able to use the drugs. Since mifepristone has only been tested since 1982, the long-term health risks aren't known. Mifepristone has a failure rate of about 4%.

Emotions
(continued)

. . . relieved that the pregnancy is over. Other girls have conflicting feelings, making the decision difficult and even painful. This is often the case when the girl's boyfriend, family, or friends don't support her decision for personal or religious reasons, or when she herself has personal or religious beliefs that don't support it. When the pregnancy is over, these girls can experience bouts of guilt, sadness, or depression, even over a long period.

Q: If I want to try total abstinence, does that mean I can't even masturbate?

A: What are you looking for from total abstinence? If it's about not being sexual with a partner, then you can masturbate comfortably without imposing on that goal. If it's about not exploring or acting on sexual desire in any way, then you'll feel more comfortable if you don't masturbate.

Q: Does being abstinent mean a person is frigid?

A: Not at all. Guys and girls who decide not to have sex are as capable of feeling sexual excitement and having an orgasm as the next person. For any number of reasons, they've decided to put sex on the back burner. Anyway, the term frigid is out of date, unless you're talking about a lake in early spring. See Frigidity.

Q: What if people think I'm weird because I want to be abstinent?

A: It's up to you to make decisions that are right for you regardless of what anyone else thinks. There will always be people who don't like what you do, no matter what you choose. Better to have a few people think you're weird than to do something you'll regret.

Abstinence
↘celibacy
↘chastity

Choosing abstinence, whether for spiritual, religious, or pragmatic reasons, means choosing not to have sex. There are 2 kinds of abstinence:

↘Total abstinence is when you decide not to take part in any sexual activities at all with another person. This is the only sure way of avoiding infection with HIV and other sexually transmitted infections. For some people total abstinence even means not kissing.

↘Partial abstinence is when you decide not to have intercourse but you still participate in other sexual activities such as kissing or mutual masturbation. Teens who practise this kind of abstinence get to enjoy the pleasures of being sexual with a partner, even to the point of orgasm, while knowing they're at lower risk of contracting most sexually transmitted infections. Whether you choose total or partial abstinence, you have the advantage of knowing there's no risk of pregnancy as long as semen doesn't go near the opening to the vagina.

Figuring out whether or not you're ready to start having sex can be hard. Pressure from friends to "do it" can make you feel rushed and uncomfortable. Or maybe you're worried about the way your partner will act afterwards. One of the good things about abstinence is that it buys you time to discover what's right for you. It also gives you a chance to prepare for the emotions, thoughts, and responsibilities that come into play once you become sexually active. Some people choose abstinence for short periods, others choose it until they find a partner they really love or can commit to for life.

Q: Isn't it unhealthy to ignore sexual urges?

A: It's not a good idea to ignore your sexual urges, but it is a good idea to understand them and control them and only act on them in appropriate situations. If you're horny and you can't do anything about it, either with a partner or by masturbating, try thinking about something else and the feeling will eventually disappear. It won't hurt you to hold off until the timing is right.

Q: Is it possible to try abstinence even if you've already had sex?

A: Anyone can try abstinence for any amount of time, even non-virgins.

Q: What if I really like someone but don't feel ready for sex?

A: It's normal to hold off on sex until you feel good about it. In the meantime, let the person know how you feel and see where it goes from there. Sexual intercourse may be out of the question, but that doesn't mean you can't practise your kissing skills. Who knows, maybe the person you like feels the same way. See Ready for Sex.

Contrary to what you might hear, not all guys are ready to have sex anytime, anywhere, with anyone. What feels right for some guys is to not get involved with sex at all, at least for the time being.

Abusive Relationships

It's sometimes hard to know when you're in an abusive relationship. Everyone gets angry over small things from time to time, often because they're unable to talk about what they really feel. Outbursts that are infrequent may be unpleasant, but they can also be a starting point for learning. Behaviour that's abusive is usually more constant, more direct, or more severe. No matter how in love you feel, it's important to end your relationship if your boyfriend or girlfriend does any of the following: constantly criticizes you, gets angry at you repeatedly over small things, tries to control who you see and what you do, makes fun of you in front of other people, acts very jealous or ignores you, likes to scare or humiliate you, makes you do sexual things you don't want to do, threatens to hit or hurt you, hurts you physically, or becomes violent after using drugs or alcohol. It's also abusive if the person you like doesn't care about your needs, but is only interested in making sure his or her needs are met.

No one has the right to control, hurt, or ignore you. Like everyone, you deserve to be treated with affection, care, and respect. Don't settle for anything less.

How to stop it

Keep looking until you find someone you can talk to about your relationship. Perhaps a friend, a parent, a favourite aunt or uncle, your family doctor, a guidance counsellor, a community nurse, or a member of the clergy will be able to help. If there's no one you can trust, you can call one of the help line numbers at the back of this book. Whoever answers will be sympathetic and able to help.

Adolescence

These are the years between childhood and adulthood when your body goes through the changes of puberty and you first become aware of sexual thoughts and feelings. During adolescence, you learn to cope with new emotions and relationships by fantasizing, having crushes, and experimenting socially and sexually. As peers become more important, so does the need to fit in. Pressure from peers to conform leads many teenagers to try new sexual behaviours. The results are sometimes thrilling; at other times, trying something new before you're ready can lead to confusion or hurt feelings. Everyone becomes sexually active at a different pace. Adolescence is easier if you accept and respect your pace and communicate your boundaries honestly to the people around you.

Age of Consent

In England, Wales and Scotland, the age of consent is 16 for heterosexual vaginal sex, and in Northern Ireland, 17. Girls who have sex before reaching the age of consent aren't considered to be acting illegally because the law says they aren't capable of giving consent. Whatever age a guy thinks a girl is, it's an absolute offence for him to have sex with a girl under the age of 13, or 14 in Northern Ireland, which is called "unlawful sexual intercourse." If the man is over 24, he faces a life sentence in prison (the question of consent isn't taken into consideration, so the act is qualified as rape). If a guy has sex with a girl between 14 and 16, this is classified as either "rape without consent" or "unlawful sexual intercourse with consent." He faces a maximum sentence of life in prison for rape, or 2 years for unlawful sexual intercourse. A 14 or 15-year-old male having consensual sex with a 14 or 15-year-old female is illegal, but in most cases considered less serious. However, the male might still be charged with a sexual offence, for which he could be placed on the sex offenders register.

In England and Wales, the age of consent for heterosexual anal sex is 16. It is not an offence in Scotland, but in Northern Ireland it is still illegal under common law. The age of consent for anal sex between men is 16 in England, Wales and Scotland, 17 in Northern Ireland, and 21 in the Isle of Man.

Q: How can you tell if someone has HIV?

A: HIV can exist in someone's body without any symptoms for up to 10 years. In other words, there are a lot of people walking around who look good and feel great, but are infected with HIV. Many of them don't realize it, so you should always use protection. In some cases, people know they're HIV-positive, but they keep it a secret. Maybe they're embarrassed by it or too afraid to talk about it. Because some people lie about having the virus, being told by your partner that he or she is HIV-negative is no guarantee. The only way you can be sure that someone is HIV-negative is to get tested together after you've been in a monogamous relationship with that person for 6 months. During those 6 months, always use a condom.

You can't get AIDS or HIV from giving blood because the needle used in the process is brand new and sterile. When the needle is taken out of your arm it's immediately thrown away.

AIDS

↘Acquired Immune Deficiency Syndrome

Before you can be diagnosed with AIDS, first you have to become infected with HIV, the human immunodeficiency virus. Once you're infected, the virus lives in your blood, and over many years weakens your immune and nervous systems. During these years you'll have almost no symptoms, so unless you've been diagnosed as HIV-positive, there's a good chance you won't know there's anything wrong. In the United Kingdom, you are only considered to have AIDS when your immune system becomes so weak that you get really sick and develop one of a number of particularly severe illnesses. See HIV.

AIDS-related illnesses

These are illnesses that typically develop in people whose immune systems are severely damaged by HIV. They include PCP (a deadly form of pneumonia), tuberculosis, Kaposi's sarcoma (a skin cancer), non-Hodgkin's lymphoma, herpes simplex, and many others.

Treatment

There's still no cure for AIDS and no vaccine for HIV. In the meantime, drugs have been developed to fight HIV in the bloodstream, significantly slowing its progress. The result is an immune system that stays strong longer. The drugs—called anti-virals or "cocktails"—are given to people with HIV in combinations of 3, so that if one stops working, the other 2 keep up the fight until a new drug is developed that will replace the old one. In this way researchers are hoping to turn AIDS from a deadly disease into a chronic one that people can live with for decades.

Unfortunately, cocktails have such negative side effects in some people that they have to stop taking them. In other people, they don't work at all. Even for people who can live with the side effects, taking cocktails isn't easy. The drugs have to be ingested in a rigid order at specific times with certain foods or fluids. Missing even 1 pill can result in an immunity to that drug.

Availability of treatment

When cocktails that combat HIV are combined with medications that treat AIDS-related diseases, the result is improved health and a better quality of life. But all these drugs are very costly. In the United Kingdom, treatment with anti-HIV drugs costs c. £10,000 per year. The average lifetime treatment cost for each HIV-positive individual is estimated to be £130,000 to £181,000.

UNICEF reports that every minute, 6 people between the ages of 15 and 24 become infected with HIV.

More than 7,000 new HIV infections occur worldwide each day. About 90% of these are the result of heterosexual sex.

In the U.K., over 3,000 children and teenagers have been diagnosed with HIV or AIDS.

Botswana has the world's highest rate of HIV infection. Right now, life expectancy in Botswana is 39. Without AIDS it would be 71.

Q & A

Q: Can a person become infected with HIV while performing oral sex?

A: Yes. Performing oral sex is less risky than sexual intercourse, but it's not risk-free. If your partner is an infected male, the virus will be present in his semen, and to a lesser degree, in his pre-ejaculate. If she's an infected female, she'll have HIV in her menstrual blood, and a smaller amount in her vaginal fluids. Sores or tiny cuts in your mouth can allow HIV to enter your bloodstream. To be safer, use a condom or a dam when performing oral sex.

Q: I know a person can contract HIV while giving oral sex, but what about while receiving it?

A: There are no recorded cases of anyone becoming infected with HIV while receiving oral sex, probably due to the fact that the amount of HIV in someone's saliva is too small to infect another person. But it's possible to catch other sexually transmitted infections by receiving oral sex, so it's always a good idea to use a condom or dam. The safer you feel, the more open you'll be to the sensations of oral pleasure.

Alcohol

↘beer   ↘pints

↘wine

↘liquor

When you're making decisions about sex—how far you want to go, who you want to be with, what protection is available—you need to be clear-headed and honest with yourself. Drinking alcohol gets in the way of that. By lowering your inhibitions, boosting your self-confidence, and slowing your reflexes, alcohol interferes with your ability to think clearly and make decisions that respect you and your partner. This happens in a shorter time to girls, who tend to get drunk faster than guys due to their physical makeup.

People drink for all kinds of reasons—to loosen up, to feel on top of it, to fit in, to have a wild time. One of the downsides of drinking is that you're more likely to end up doing sexual things that you wouldn't do if you were sober. Afterwards you may feel stupid, embarrassed, angry, hurt, or scared, especially if you can't remember what you did. Being drunk can also make you more vulnerable to pressure, and to putting the pressure on someone else. The worst-case scenario is that you have sex, and because you're drunk, you laugh off the idea of protection. Later you find out you're pregnant, or that your girlfriend is pregnant. Or maybe you discover you're infected with HIV or another sexually transmitted infection.

Ironically, even though guys may feel hornier when they're intoxicated, alcohol actually decreases their ability to perform: erections are harder to get, and if you get one, it may not last long.

Anal Sex

↘ sodomy

↘ buggery

This is when an erect penis enters the rectum of a partner through the anus. Because the lower rectum is usually empty, this isn't as messy as you might think. For some couples—homosexual and hetero-sexual—anal sex is a turn-on. After all, it stimulates the many nerve endings that surround the anus. For others, it's the last thing in the world they want to do. Because the rectum doesn't stretch as much as the vagina, penetration (no more than an inch or 2) should be gentle to avoid tearing and pain. Using plenty of lubrication is important, as is being relaxed. But if you don't want to do it, just tell your partner. Anal sex may not be your idea of a good time, and that's fair. Practised regularly over a long period, anal sex can stretch the anal sphincter and lead to incontinence (not being able to control your bowel movements).

Sometimes the anus can also be stimulated by sliding one or more fingers, or even a small object, into it. Bear in mind that using an object can be hazardous because it may get stuck. No matter what you're inserting, don't forget to wash it with soap and water before putting it near your partner's vagina, mouth or urethra. While certain germs live naturally and healthily in the anus, when introduced to other areas of the body, an infection may follow. See Age of Consent, Rimming.

Q & A

Q: Is anal sex safer than vaginal sex?

A: While only vaginal sex can lead to pregnancy, anal sex has a higher risk of passing on HIV and other infections. The lining of the rectum is more delicate than the lining of the vagina, and can tear and bleed more easily, allowing viruses to enter the receiver's bloodstream. Since infected blood contains a higher concentration of HIV than infected vaginal fluids, anal sex also places the giver at a higher risk.

Q: Is it immoral to have anal sex?

A: No part of your body, including your anus, is inherently dirty or immoral. From head to toe the human body is a sexual landscape, capable of giving and receiving pleasure in different ways. For many people, male and female, anal sex is a normal, exciting part of lovemaking. However, there are many other people who abide by religions that say anal sex is wrong. In some US states, for example, anal sex is still prohibited by law, even between consenting adults. As with so much else, you have to come to your own decision about what you think is moral.

Anal sex on its own can't lead to infection with the AIDS virus (HIV). For you to contract the virus, your partner has to already be infected. The same is true of all sexually transmitted infections. Anal sex doesn't cause them.

It's not true that anal sex is the only part of gay male sexual activity. Some men like it, but lots don't.

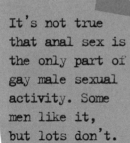

STIs you can get

- HIV
- herpes
- gonorrhoea
- hepatitis B
- chlamydia
- syphilis
- genital warts

Protection

If you don't use a condom, anal sex is very risky. The rectum is fragile and tears and bleeds easily, allowing HIV in semen to enter the bloodstream of the receiver. To be as safe as possible, wear a condom, or better yet 2 condoms, one on top of the other. Using a water-based lubricant will decrease the possibility of breakage.

Wearing condoms will also protect the person who's giving the anal sex from his partner's blood. If the receiver's blood has HIV in it, the virus could enter the giver through his urethra, or through sores or cuts on his penis.

Condoms will also protect both partners from most other sexually transmitted infections. New research shows that injecting a spermicide made with nonoxynol-9 into the anus offers no protection against HIV and may actually increase the risk of becoming infected by it. **See Condoms, Lubricants.**

Androgynous

At first glance, most people can be identified as male or female. But there are people who have such a blend of male and female characteristics that when you look at them, you ask yourself—is he a she, or is she a he? That person could be described as androgynous. Some people cultivate an androgynous style because it's fashionable or comfortable, or because they don't feel particularly "masculine" or "feminine." For others, being androgynous is a physical reality—they were born with a combination of male and female sex parts.

In recent times, female and male roles have become far less strictly defined. For example, many guys are more openly nurturing and perceptive about feelings (behaviours that were traditionally female), and many girls are comfortably independent and competitive (behaviours that were traditionally male). Forty years ago, someone expressing a mixture of "masculine" and "feminine" behaviours might have been considered androgynous and threatening, but these days, that person is more often seen as normal. See Gender, Feminine, Hermaphrodite, Masculine.

Anus

This is the opening in your body where faeces come out. The reason this area is sensitive and so easily stimulated by touch is because it's surrounded by the same kind of nerve endings that bring pleasure to the vagina and penis. See Anal Sex, Rimming.

 Just about everyone has hair growing around their anus.

Aphrodisiacs

These are substances people ingest in the hopes of increasing or enhancing their sexual desire. They can range from the ordinary (vegetables shaped like genitalia or foods that are spicy) to the glamorous (oysters and champagne) to the grotesque (bull's testicles and goat's toenails) to the dangerous (drugs like ecstasy and speed).

Although there's no scientific proof that particular foods or drinks can actually make you feel sexier, people who believe in them insist on their magic. In other words, if you're open to being turned on by something you eat or drink, it may do the trick. Drugs, on the other hand, may create an initial feeling of excitement, but will eventually lower—if not wipe out—your feelings of sexual desire and your ability to perform. See Alcohol, Drugs.

Q & A

Q: What is Spanish fly?

A: This is a bright green beetle found in Southern Europe that is long rumoured to be an aphrodisiac. Ingesting Spanish fly (usually in powder form) irritates the urethra in a way that mimics arousal. But the effects can be more far-reaching, leading to serious abdominal pain and even death.

Q: If I don't want my girlfriend to get pregnant, can I have intercourse with her, but stop myself from ejaculating?

A: If your penis continues to receive stimulation, eventually you'll ejaculate. Even before that happens, your penis may leak pre-ejaculate into her vagina, which can contain sperm. The only sure way to avoid getting your girlfriend pregnant is to abstain from intercourse. Some forms of birth control are also very effective at preventing pregnancy. See Birth Control, Withdrawal.

To have good sexual experiences it's important to know what turns you on. The next step is to communicate this information to your partner, which is much easier to do if both of you feel safe and comfortable.

Arousal

↘getting turned on
↘getting horny
↘getting wet

This is about becoming sexually excited, not only in your body, but in your mind too. It can happen fast—the instant you see someone sexy or imagine a steamy sex scene—or over several hours as you allow yourself to be seduced by the sound of someone's voice or the way you're being treated or touched. Because everyone is different, what's sexually exciting for one person may not be a turn-on for someone else.

Arousal is essential if you're planning to have intercourse. It's during this stage that the body gets ready for penetration—the penis hardens and the vagina becomes wet. If you're not physically prepared, intercourse will be difficult. Continued arousal through physical stimulation usually leads to orgasm, especially if you're relaxed and open to it. Stimulation that's too rough will probably turn you off. Becoming fully aroused can take 5 minutes, a half hour, or longer. The length of time varies with each person, and even for you it can change from one day to the next, depending on what mood you're in. For many people, the sex play that stimulates arousal is the most satisfying part of sex, even better than climaxing.

Arousal

In females ♀

It's a fact of life that physical arousal usually takes longer in females than in males, sometimes much longer, even for the very experienced. In general it goes like this: You begin by being relaxed and open to the sensations sexual activities bring (at this stage you may or may not feel desire). Then your body receives stimulation—by being kissed, licked, stroked, sucked, rubbed, or pressed against. As the stimulation continues, your skin becomes sensitive, your heart beats faster, and your blood pressure goes up, sending a surge of blood to your genitals. By this time your vagina is getting ready to be penetrated. The lips open wide and the inside expands and becomes wet with a slippery mucus (when the vagina is wet the penis or fingers can easily slide in and out). The clitoris swells and becomes very sensitive to touch. Your nipples become erect. As you become more intensely excited, your muscles tighten and you begin to breathe faster.

By now your body is feeling hot and the skin on your chest may become slightly red. This is called a sex flush. Your vagina is very wet and the opening tightens a bit. Stimulation continues and finally you orgasm (once, twice, maybe 3 times), which is always a good feeling, and sometimes an amazing one. After orgasm your body relaxes completely. Your breathing slows down and the blood drains away from your genitals. Everything returns to normal in less than 5 minutes. If you don't orgasm and the stimulation stops, your body will still return to normal, though it will take longer. If this happens, your genitals may feel achy for a short while, until all the blood leaves the area. Many women don't orgasm and enjoy the sex anyway. See Clitoris, Desire, Orgasm.

In males ♂

In most guys arousal can happen in a matter of seconds, when a single thought or a seductive touch leads to an instant erection. Erections can even happen unexpectedly, without any sexual stimulation at all. Or a penis can be aroused in stages, starting off soft, then slowly becoming hard, then harder, as stimulation increases. Physically, arousal generally works like this: your nervous system sends messages to the arteries leading to your penis, telling them to expand (at this stage you may or may not feel desire). With the expansion of these arteries, large amounts of blood rush into the spongy cylinders that surround the penis. All this blood stiffens your penis and makes it bigger and darker in colour. At the same time, the testicles enlarge and draw closer to your body, sometimes all but disappearing. Your blood pressure goes up.

If fondling (or thrusting) continues, the muscles in your body tighten and you feel hot. You may get a slightly red rash on your chest called a sex flush. Your heart rate and breathing speed up, and a small amount of clear fluid may form on the tip of your penis. This is called pre-ejaculate. After more stimulation you ejaculate, which means your semen is propelled through your penis by uncontrollable muscle contractions. It only takes a second before it spurts out the end. Though it's not guaranteed, you'll probably orgasm at the same time. This is always a good feeling, and sometimes a great one. After ejaculation your body will return to its normal state in less than 5 minutes. If you don't ejaculate, you may feel pain in your testicles for a few hours, until everything returns to normal. **See Blue Balls, Orgasm, Pre-ejaculate.**

Bacterial Vaginosis ♀

 BV

Lots of girls get this infection. It begins when bacteria in the vagina multiply out of control. The most common symptom is a thin, greyish discharge that gives off a strong fishy odour, especially after intercourse. Often your partner will smell it first. In some girls the discharge causes irritation and a burning feeling when they pee, but this is rare. Some girls have no symptoms at all and only find out they have BV when they visit their doctor for a checkup. The bacteria that cause BV may occasionally cause an infection (pelvic inflammatory disease). This is most likely to occur after a termination of pregnancy.

Treatment

A doctor who diagnoses BV will prescribe an antibiotic in the form of pills. Girls may also have the choice of a gel or cream that's put inside the vagina. Used as instructed, the antibiotic will eliminate the problem.

Prevention

Keeping your vulva clean and dry may help you to avoid BV. Synthetic underwear, tights, lycra, and tight trousers don't allow air to circulate around the vulva. This creates a moist environment in which bacteria thrive. For daytime, white cotton underwear are best. At night, take off your undies and put on something loose and comfortable to sleep in (a nightie is ideal). This will let your vulva air out. To keep this area clean, wash daily with warm water and a mild, unscented soap. Avoid douching and too many hot baths as these can destroy the natural acidic balance in your vagina, making it more susceptible to infection. BV is not considered a sexually transmitted infection. However, some woman find they are more likely to develop BV when they are particularly sexually active. **See Douching, Yeast Infections.**

In males ♂

Males can become infected with BV bacteria, although usually there are no symptoms. Very occasionally, the bacteria can cause the penis head, foreskin or urethra to become red and sore.

10 reasons for bad sex that you can do something about

1. Your partner is interested in sex, not you. **Tell them it's over.**
2. Your partner has no idea how to please you and doesn't care. **Drop them.**
3. You're having sex because you let yourself be pressured into it. **Don't let the pressure get to you.**
4. You're worried about pregnancy. **Use birth control.**
5. You're not protected and you can't get AIDS off your mind. **Use protection.**
6. You're trying to please your partner but you have no idea what to do and you're scared to ask. **Be brave and ask; read more books on sex.**
7. You don't like your partner all that much. **End the relationship.**
8. You're not relaxed because you're afraid someone's going to walk in on you. **Choose your location more carefully.**
9. You're tense because you hate the way you look, you don't like your voice, and your hair is all wrong. **Focus on the important stuff.**
10. You feel uncomfortable about having sex in the first place. **Wait till you're ready.**

Bad Sex

↘ it–wasn't–as–much–fun–as–I–thought–it–would–be sex

Sex isn't great every time, especially when you're just starting out. It can be awkward, disappointing, embarrassing, uncomfortable, painful, or just plain boring. The important thing is to not beat yourself up about it and to learn from the experience. The better you get at making choices that are right for you—about who to be with, when and where to do it, and what kind of protection to use—the better the sex will be. The sex will also improve if you and your partner are able to communicate your thoughts, feelings, and desires to each other, maybe not all of them at once, but at least a few to start. If your choices are good ones and you and your partner trust each other and communicate well, and the sex is still just so-so, don't worry. Sex improves with practice. See Communication, Ready for Sex.

Bad Sex

In females ♀

The culprit behind bad sex is frequently a dry, tight vagina. When this happens it's not because there's something wrong with your vagina, but because for some reason you're not relaxed or aroused. Maybe it's your first time and you're nervous. Or you're self-conscious about your body and you just can't let go. Maybe you're being pressured into sex, or you and your partner are moving too fast and you're not getting the time or attention you need to become physically aroused. Arousal is essential for good sex because it's during this stage that the vagina gets wet. If everything is going okay but you're still dry, an easy solution is to lubricate yourself with a bit of K-Y jelly or another water-based lubricant. Check the shelves in the pharmacy to see what's available.
See Arousal, First Sex, Lubricants, Vaginismus.

In males ♂

For most guys bad sex means one of 3 things: ejaculating too soon, not being able to get an erection, or getting an erection but not being able to keep it. There are reasons these things happen, and they have nothing to do with your masculinity. For starters, it's normal for teenagers to ejaculate soon after stimulation begins. In fact, most teens ejaculate very soon after, largely because they haven't had much practice at sex. If you don't expect to hold out for more than 30 seconds or a minute, you won't be disappointed. But there are things you can do that will help improve your staying power.
See Ejaculation to find out what they are.

The reason behind a poor or non-existent erection could be stress or anxiety. Maybe you're intimidated by your partner. Or maybe you've just received some bad news. Too much alcohol can stop your penis from functioning properly by affecting your blood flow. Drug use can also get in the way. Despite how embarrassing it may feel, occasionally failing to get an erection doesn't mean there's something wrong with your penis, and it isn't the same as impotence.
See Alcohol, Drugs, Erection, Impotence.

Q & A

Q: How can I get my boyfriend to have sex with me?

A: If you end up having sex because you've pressured him into it, neither of you will enjoy it. To have good sex, you both have to want it and be ready for it. It will be easier to respect your boyfriend's feelings if you find out why he doesn't want to sleep with you. Ask him what he'd like to do instead. There are many ways you can enjoy each other sexually without having intercourse.

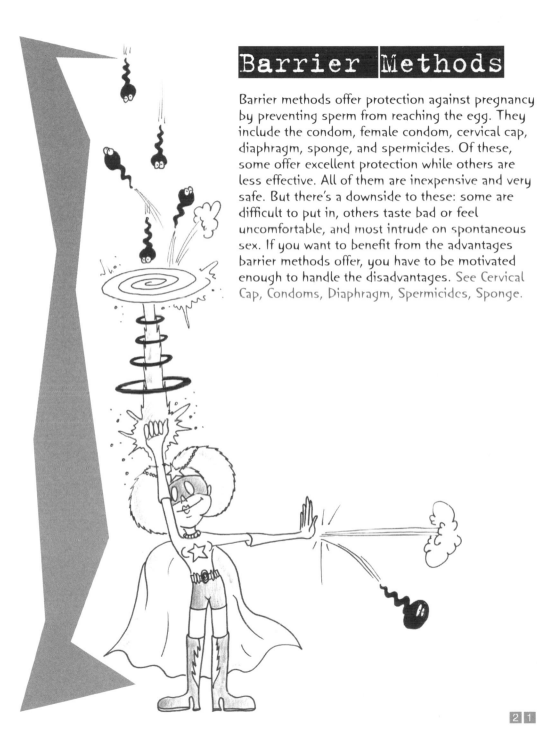

Barrier Methods

Barrier methods offer protection against pregnancy by preventing sperm from reaching the egg. They include the condom, female condom, cervical cap, diaphragm, sponge, and spermicides. Of these, some offer excellent protection while others are less effective. All of them are inexpensive and very safe. But there's a downside to these: some are difficult to put in, others taste bad or feel uncomfortable, and most intrude on spontaneous sex. If you want to benefit from the advantages barrier methods offer, you have to be motivated enough to handle the disadvantages. See Cervical Cap, Condoms, Diaphragm, Spermicides, Sponge.

Birth Control ♀
↘contraception

Over 115,000 teenage girls get pregnant every year in the United Kingdom. The majority of these pregnancies are completely unexpected, despite the fact that most girls know that sex can lead to pregnancy. Sex can always lead to pregnancy, so you always have to use birth control if you don't want to get pregnant.

The first step is to admit to yourself that you're gearing up for sex. The next step is to make a decision to be responsible about it. Then it's time to check out the different birth control methods available on the market. When you find one that appeals to you, some questions you should ask are: how often does it fail? is it easy to use? does it protect against HIV or other sexually transmitted infections? is it affordable? how can I get it? are there any side effects? You also need to talk about birth control with your partner. If you're both comfortable with the method you choose, you're more likely to use it correctly and consistently. If you do all this, you stand a good chance of avoiding pregnancy.

Birth control methods that stop a pregnancy from getting started by changing hormone levels in the female body include the birth control pill, mini-pill, Implanon (a hormonal implant), and Depo-Provera. Birth control methods that stop sperm from reaching the egg are called barrier methods and include the condom, the female condom,* the diaphragm, the cervical cap, the sponge, and spermicides. Other birth control methods are the IUD and the rhythm method, but the last one is extremely unreliable. As a last resort, emergency contraception will significantly lower your risk of getting pregnant.

It takes 2 to tango, so don't assume it's the girl's responsibility to worry about preventing pregnancy. If you're not sure whether she's using contraception, play it safe and wear a condom. In a long-term relationship, you can offer to share any costs related to birth control.

Birth Control

Of all the birth control methods, only 2 offer protection from HIV and sexually transmitted infections: the condom and the female condom. Until recently, spermicides were thought to provide protection from HIV, but a new report indicates that one type, Nonoxynol-9, may actually increase the risk of becoming infected with the virus.

The ultimate birth control method is abstinence, which is 100% effective. Abstinence demands that you give up penis-vagina sex and any activities that leave sperm close to the vaginal opening. But it doesn't mean you can't explore the dozens of other ways people give and receive sexual pleasure in a loving relationship. The birth control method that is final—sterilization through surgery—isn't usually recommended for teenagers. See Abstinence, Barrier Methods, Birth Control Pill, Cervical Cap, Condoms, Depo-Provera, Diaphragm, Emergency Contraception, IUD, Rhythm Method, Spermicides, Sponge.

↘ Lots of girls won't insist on birth control if the guy they're sleeping with doesn't want to use it. The opposite also happens, where guys want to use birth control but won't push the issue if their girlfriend says she doesn't want it.

↘ One in 4 girls will get pregnant in the first month of having unprotected intercourse.

↘ Many teenagers don't inform themselves about birth control because they don't want to admit to anyone, even themselves, that they're interested in having sex. Others would be comfortable using birth control, but don't because they're afraid their parents will find out.

Parental consent

Individuals under the age of 16 may receive contraception if they are considered competent to consent to medical treatment (that is, if they can show they are able to fully understand what is being proposed). A doctor providing contraception to a person under 16 would strongly advise the individual to discuss the matter with a parent, but would also respect the patient's confidentiality – they can only disclose information to the parent with the child's consent. Most doctors will provide contraception if they feel it is in the best interests of the individual and are comfortable that the individual fully appreciates the issues involved.

Birth Control Pill

the Pill

The Pill is one of the most effective birth control methods on the market, stopping pregnancy 99.9% of the time if you use it right. It works by introducing 2 synthetic hormones into your body. The first hormone is oestrogen. It does 2 things: tells the ovaries to stop producing eggs, and thins the lining of the uterus so that a fertilized egg can't settle there. The second hormone is progestogen. It thickens the mucus that plugs the cervix, making it more difficult for sperm to enter the uterus. Some brands of the Pill only contain progestogen and are slightly less effective than the oestrogen-progestogen combination.

How to use it

The Pill isn't recommended if your period is still irregular, but if you're having sex frequently, it might be wise to go on it anyway. Discuss this with your doctor. If you've decided the Pill is right for you, take it every day at the same time (pick something you do day after day, like brushing your teeth in the morning, and use that as a reminder). This makes it a good choice if you're a disciplined person. If you forget to take a pill or 2, there's a way of catching up. Just call your doctor or pharmacist and ask what to do. The Pill can be used long-term, even until menopause, unless you're a smoker. Women who smoke are advised to stop taking it at 35. If they keep taking the Pill, there's a greater chance they'll suffer a stroke or heart attack, or form blood clots.

Q & A

Q: Will taking the Pill make me fat?

A: Studies show that some women gain a bit of weight from going on the Pill. This isn't due to the number of calories in the Pill, but to the fact that your appetite may increase in the first few months of being on it. If you don't change what you eat and you keep to your regular exercise routine, you won't gain weight. Some women actually lose weight.

Q: Is it true that you have to take a break from the Pill once in a while to let your body return to normal?

A: It's not true. Once your body is used to the Pill, you should keep on taking it to avoid irregular cycles. Using it in short bursts will only upset your reproductive system, leaving you vulnerable to pregnancy.

24

Birth Control Pill

Availability

The Pill is a prescribed medication, which means you need a prescription to buy it. To get a prescription, it's necessary to see your family doctor, or attend a family planning or sexual health clinic. An examination is not usually required. Prescribed contraception is free in the UK.

Advantages

Extremely effective and very easy to use. Women like not having to worry about contraception every time they have sex. Affects menstrual flow in ways women appreciate, by making it lighter, more regular, and less painful. Once in a while some women even miss a period altogether (this is nothing to worry about unless they forgot to take one of the pills, in which case they might be pregnant). Other advantages: women feel good knowing they can stop the Pill anytime and get pregnant if they want to (unless they have unrelated problems with fertility); it offers protection against pelvic inflammatory disease; in some cases the Pill reduces acne; women on the Pill have fewer ovarian cysts and breast diseases, and they're less likely to get infected fallopian tubes or to have an ectopic pregnancy; and taking the Pill over several years lowers the risk of ovarian and endometrial cancer.

Disadvantages

Offers no protection from HIV or other sexually transmitted infections, which is why women on the Pill should still use a condom every time they have sex. If you forget to take even 1 pill, you might become pregnant. Some women experience nausea and unexpected bleeding when they first start taking it (these side effects usually disappear after the first 3 cycles, when the body gets used to its new routine). Other side effects that occur in some women include bloating, slight weight gain or loss, skin problems, sore and sometimes swollen breasts, reduced sexual desire, and depression. Trying a different brand of pill may reduce or eliminate these symptoms.

More serious side effects include dizziness or very bad headaches, numbness, blurred vision, and swollen, painful legs. If you experience any of these, stop taking the Pill immediately and see your doctor or go to an Accident and Emergency department. Finally, it's possible that using the Pill will slightly increase your chances of getting breast cancer, though it's unclear whether this is true or not.

Bisexual

↳swing both ways

This word describes a girl or guy who's sexually attracted to both females and males, though not necessarily at the same time. Realizing you're bisexual can be a process that unfolds over time or it can happen suddenly, either in your teens or later in life. Being bisexual can mean many things, including having same-sex activities while fantasizing about the other sex; being in a good sexual relationship with someone of the opposite sex for many years, then suddenly falling in love with someone of the same sex, or vice versa; or being sexually involved with members of both sexes over a period of years. Many people who experience bisexuality end up settling down for good in either a gay or straight relationship.

Unfortunately, there are lots of people in the world who believe that same-sex activities are immoral. Though many others believe this to be untrue, the negative attitudes of people around you can be hurtful. If you're confused about your sexual orientation but think you may be bisexual or gay, tell your feelings to someone you can trust. If you can't think of anyone among your family or friends, try calling a telephone help line. Talking about your sexual feelings doesn't mean you have to act on them, but it could help you to feel less isolated.

Q&A

Q: Is it okay if I'm bisexual?

A: It's more than okay. It's smart and healthy to be the person you really are.

On its own, experimenting sexually with both guys and girls doesn't mean you're bisexual. Nor does having fantasies or being curious about members of both sexes. How a person behaves and feels sexually over time is a stronger indication of bisexuality.

See Gay, Heterosexual, Homosexual, Lesbian, Queer.

A: Some people believe that "blue balls" originates in the epididymis, the tiny, very long tube inside the scrotum that sperm pass through after they leave the testicles and before they're ejected into the urethra. When sperm exit the testicles but aren't sent shooting through the urethra in ejaculation, they get backed up in the epididymis. This causes pain.

Blue Balls ♂

This expression describes the soreness or pain guys feel in their testicles when they've had an erection for a long time but for one reason or another don't ejaculate. Some guys will even beg their partners to have sex with them, claiming their "blue balls" are killing them. But it's never that bad, and girlfriends or boyfriends shouldn't feel obliged to do anything they don't want to do. The painful feeling of blue balls gradually diminishes as sexual excitement dies down, then disappears. Though it can take an hour or 2 for the pain to go away, no harm will come to the penis or testicles. If you've got blue balls and want immediate relief, your best bet is to masturbate.

Breasts

- ↘ boobs
- ↘ tits
- ↘ knockers
- ↘ melons
- ↘ jugs
- ↘ hooters

Most girls, and some guys, look at female breasts and see 2 mounds of flesh—small, medium, or large—each topped by a nipple. Nice, but nothing to get excited about. Most guys, and some girls, look at female breasts and see uncharted territory and untold pleasures. Everything to get excited about! Babies see a source of nourishment, warmth, and comfort. Owners—the women behind the breasts—like the feeling of having them caressed. Breasts, it seems, offer something for just about everyone.

In females ♀

What about your own breasts? Are they still growing? It takes about 5 years for breasts to reach their final size. Is one slightly larger than the other? That's true for many girls, in the same way that one foot or one eye can be larger than the other? Are they bigger than you'd like them to be, or too small? You don't have any control over

Q&A

Q: What can I do about the hair that's growing around my nipples?

A: Many girls have hair growing on their breasts, usually around the areola. If you want, you can trim it, tweeze it, or remove it permanently through electrolysis. If there are only a few strands, you can ignore them. Girls on the Pill sometimes discover new hairs growing on their breasts.

Q: Are there exercises girls can do to make their breasts bigger?

A: There's no muscle in breasts, which means there's nothing to exercise to make bigger. The most you can do is exercise the pectoral muscles that sit under your breasts.

Q & A

Q: Are girls with big breasts hornier than girls with small ones?

A: Breast size has nothing to do with a girl's level of sexual desire. She can be flat-chested and feel hot, or big-breasted and feel completely unready for sexual involvement. You'll learn more about girls by observing their actions, not their cup size.

Q: When should I start wearing a bra?

A: You'll know when you're ready. For some girls, it's when their nipples stick out, making them feel self-conscious. For others, it's when their breasts become too heavy to dance or play sports comfortably. For lots of girls, it's time to get a bra when all their friends get one. Then there are girls who are more comfortable without a bra, and settle on undershirts or nothing at all.

the way your breasts develop, but you can control how you feel about them. A good place to start is by realizing that all breasts are beautiful, regardless of their shape and size. The reason many girls don't like their breasts is because they compare them to the make-believe breasts they see on film and in advertisements. But those breasts are manufactured images that have nothing to do with reality. If you think about it, anyone who's turned on by real-life breasts pretty much likes all breasts.

Breasts can be pointy or round, perky or heavy, huge or teeny tiny, or anything in between. To understand what's behind these differences, you have to look at family history and fat. Not body fat, but the fatty tissue that's destined to be in your breasts due to the genes you inherited from your father and mother. In other words, how your breasts look has nothing to do with your intelligence or sexual awareness or sense of humour, and everything to do with how much fatty tissue is programmed to accumulate there. If it's a lot, you'll have big breasts; if it's only a bit, you'll have small ones.

All breasts, whether they're flat or mountainous, are very sensitive to touch (though some women like being fondled there more than others). This sensitivity is due to the fact that they all hold about the same number of nerve endings. Besides nerve endings and fatty tissue, each breast contains 15 to 20 clusters of mammary glands. When a woman gives birth, these glands produce milk for her new baby.

Breasts develop in puberty when the body starts to produce oestrogen (a hormone). The oestrogen stimulates the fatty tissue to grow. Girls with more fatty tissue end up with larger breasts than girls with less fatty tissue. Some girls don't like having large, eye-catching breasts because it makes them feel self-conscious, especially if they're the target of jokes. Others find big breasts inconvenient. Not only can they make it hard to play sports or do any kind of vigorous activity, they can also be a source of pain (in the back, neck, and shoulders), as well as rashes. If they can afford it, some women in this situation have an operation to make their breasts smaller. Because the operation is permanent and involves risk, discomfort, and scarring, most women think carefully before having it.

Breasts aren't unchanging. They swell a bit during sexual excitement. In some girls, they become full and tender just before their period starts and stay that way until it's over.

Breasts

Most girls' breasts feel different depending on the time of month. Actually, it's the lumps in the breast that feel different. Breasts are lumpy because of their fatty tissue. This lumpiness may change slightly as the menstrual cycle progresses. If you discover a lump that stays the same for several weeks, ask a doctor to check it out. Most breast lumps aren't cancer, but some are. A soreness in your breast may mean you have an infection. See a doctor about it.

Breast self-examination

There are good habits and bad ones. Examining your breasts for unusual lumps is a good habit, even a neces sary one. This is because breast cancer is a female reality. Though it rarely shows up in teenagers, 1 woman in 9 will develop breast cancer sometime in her life. If it's treated early, there's a better chance it will be cured. But it has to be found early. That's where the breast self-examination comes in. It should be done every month just after the end of your period, but only once your breasts are fully grown, which usually happens around 18. The better you know your breasts, the easier it will be to detect a problem should there ever be one.

There are 2 ways to do the check yourself. They both involve using your 3 middle fingers, which you keep straight and close together. As you feel your breasts, use the pads of your fingers, not the fingertips. Check for new lumps or unfamiliar thick areas.

1. It's easy to examine your breasts during a shower, when soapy fingers glide smoothly across the skin. Put your left hand behind your head. Use your right hand to feel your left breast. Starting at the top of your breast, use small circular motions to feel all the way down to your nipple. Do this over the entire breast, always start-ing at the outside and moving in. When you're done, check under your armpit, where there is also breast tissue. Now do the right breast, using your left hand.

Q & A

Q: Are breast implants safe or not?

A: There are risks to getting implants: the implant could break apart inside your body, you could develop painful scar tissue, and you could have less feeling in your breast. There's also a chance the implant will gradually shift its position. All of these things have happened to many women with breast implants. Other suspected risks include cancer, disorders related to the immune system, and problems with breastfeeding.

Q: What should I do if one of my breasts is much smaller than the other?

A: If your breasts are still developing, there's a good chance the smaller one will catch up in size. If it doesn't, you can slip a pad into your bra on the side with the smaller breast. Just about all girls have different-sized breasts, but the truth is, no one notices.

Q & A ♂

Q: I'm a guy, and when I was 11, I got bumps under my nipples. I thought I was getting breasts! Then the bumps went away. What happened?

A: It's very common for boys in puberty to develop a lump just under each nipple. These lumps are caused by female hormones that are produced in the male body in small amounts starting in puberty. When the male hormones kick in, the lumps disappear, though it can take a few months.

2. For this one, put a bit of body lotion on your fingers for easier movement. Lie on your back with a pillow under your left shoulder. Place your left hand behind your head. Use your right hand to feel your left breast. Starting at your armpit, gently press your fingers down to feel the tissue between your skin and chest wall. Using small circular motions, slowly move your fingers to the top of your breast, then around to the other side, then along the bottom and back to where you started. Move your fingers an inch toward your nipple and go around your breast again. Keep this up until you've covered the whole area, including the nipple. End by feeling under your armpit, though first, bring your left arm down to your side. Do the same for the right breast, using your left hand.

Either before or after examining yourself with your fingers, take a few minutes to check your breasts in the mirror. Stand with your arms relaxed at your sides. Look for any changes. Are the size and shape the same? Is there any dimpling on the skin? Any swelling? Do your nipples look like they usually do? When you squeeze your nipples, does any fluid come out? Now raise your arms over your head and look for the same things. Lastly, put your hands on your hips and flex your chest muscles. Ask a doctor to check out anything that's unusual.

In males ♂

Guys have breasts too, just not very big ones. The small size of male breasts doesn't mean they're insensitive to touch. For many guys, breasts are definitely an erogenous zone, thanks to the fact that each breast has as many nerve endings in it as female breasts do. As a result, during sexual excitement, breasts swell a bit. Because male breasts have a small amount of actual breast tissue, it's possible for a man to get breast cancer, though this is extremely rare.

Cancer

Cancers that attack the reproductive system rarely develop in teenagers, and the ones that do can easily be detected early. Early detection and treatment increase the chances of stopping these cancers in their tracks and eliminating them from the body.

In females

There are 2 kinds of cancer you have to pay attention to: cervical cancer and breast cancer. While there's almost no chance you'll develop either of these diseases if you're under 20, you could get them when you're older, and now is the time to get into the habit of watching for them. Other types of reproductive cancers—ovarian, uterine, endometrial—only occur as women age. Research shows that taking the Pill, even as a young woman, protects against the later development of ovarian and endometrial cancer.

Cervical cancer

Cervical cancer is now thought to be caused by human papillomavirus (HPV), though the majority of women with HPV infection of the cervix never develop any abnormalities. Fortunately, if a person is predisposed to develop cancer, it can take a long time to develop – up to 15 years. This means there is time to detect and eliminate the early warning signs. These signs come in the form of dysplasia, which means abnormal cell growth. Cells that are abnormal are removed from the cervix, thus removing the potential for cancer.

You're at greater risk of developing abnormal cells if your first intercourse was at an early age, if you've had several male sexual partners, and if you smoke cigarettes or are exposed to cigarette smoke. The way to detect abnormal cells is to have a cervical smear. In the United Kingdom, women are advised to have a cervical smear at 20, then at 3-to-4-year intervals if no abnormalities are detected. **See Cervical Smear, Cervix.**

In females:

BREAST CANCER

Even though there's only a small chance you'll discover a cancerous lump in your breast, it's important to get into the habit of examining your breasts as soon as they're fully developed. Early detection has saved the lives of many women. See Breasts (Breast self-examination).

It's not unusual for teenage girls (and guys) to develop a sore, swollen spot right under one or both of their nipples. If this happens, have it checked out by a doctor. It's probably only an adolescent nodule and not breast cancer, but you have to make sure. Adolescent nodules are common in teenagers and disappear by themselves.

In males:

TESTICULAR CANCER

Pay attention to your testicles. Though testicular cancer is rare, it's the most common cancer in men under 35, including teenagers. Fortunately, it's almost always curable if found early. All guys 15 and over are advised to check their testicles on a regular basis. Other types of reproductive cancers—penile and prostate—only occur as men age. See Testicles.

Canker sores

Don't confuse these with cold sores. Cankers are small, whitish ulcers that sometimes appear in the mouth and under the tongue. They aren't caused by a virus and they're not contagious. Canker sores are usually a result of stress, fatigue, or an allergy, and will go away within a week or 2. However, because HIV and hepatitis B enter the bloodstream through cuts and open sores, be careful to practise safer sex if you have a canker sore in your mouth. See Safer Sex.

Castration

This is an operation that removes the testicles from the scrotum. We don't hear much about castration anymore, but once upon a time it was almost common. It was done as a ceremonial ritual in ancient Egypt; to keep harem guards on the straight and narrow (castrated men were called eunuchs); to preserve the high, sweet voices of choirboys; to take the "fight" out of prisoners of war; and in the United Kingdom in the 1800s, as a "cure" for masturbation and insanity. These days castration is most commonly performed as a treatment for prostate cancer, a disease that mainly afflicts men over 50.

Cervical Cap ♀

This is a small cup some women use to prevent pregnancy. Made of soft plastic or latex, it's placed deep inside the vagina, where it sits tightly over the cervix so sperm can't enter the uterus. If it's used properly every time you have sex, your chances of avoiding pregnancy are just over 90%.

To use a cervical cap properly, you must: fill it about half full with spermicide before putting it in; insert it perfectly; avoid knocking it out of place while you're making love; put more spermicide in the vagina every time you "do it" (without moving the cap); keep the cap in for at least 8 hours after the last time you have sex; and not douche, swim, or take a bath while it's in place.

One problem with cervical caps is that they only come in 4 sizes, which means they fit about 50% of women. Your doctor will examine you to determine which size is right for you. Never borrow a friend's cap because it probably won't fit. Unfortunately, cervical caps offer almost no protection against most sexually transmitted infections.

Advantages

Can be put in up to a day and a half before having sex. Can be left in for a total of 2 days (some doctors say 3 days). Has almost no side effects. Is inexpensive. Is easy to care for and store. Will be good for about 2 years.

Disadvantages

Offers some protection against chlamydia and gonorrhoea, but almost none against other sexually transmitted infections. Can be hard to put in and take out. Can get knocked off the cervix, leaving the way clear for sperm to enter the uterus. Has to be refitted if your weight changes. Some girls can't be fitted with one. The spermicide may cause an allergic reaction. Leaving it in too long can lead to foul-smelling discharge, or it can even lead to toxic shock syndrome, though this is very rare.

Availability

This method of contraception isn't used very often in the United Kingdom, but it can still be obtained free of charge from family planning centres.

♀

If you're wearing a cervical cap correctly and the guy you're with is wearing a condom, your chances of avoiding pregnancy are almost 100%. Cervical caps also offer some protection against STIs.

Cervix ♀

If you're female, one way to get to know yourself better is to explore the inside of your vagina with your finger. If you reach in far enough, you'll touch something that feels like the tip of your nose. That's the cervix. It connects your vagina to your uterus. In the center of the cervix is the os, an opening so small that only 3 things can get through it: germs, sperm, and menstrual flow. Actually, there's one exception. During childbirth, the os stretches enough for a baby to pass through.

Cervical Smear ♀
↘smear test

When you turn 20, your family doctor will contact you to make an appointment to have a cervical smear. This may be performed by the practice nurse. Cervical smears are recommended every 3 to 4 years. If abnormalities are detected, a repeat will be requested in 6 months. Women with persisting abnormalities are referred on to a gynae-cologist. Most abnormalities are due to a short-term infection with human papillomavirus. However, treatment is only recommended for abnormalities more advanced than HPV infection, which in some cases may progress over a period of several years to cervical pre-cancer and cancer. The cervical smear is a simple test, but what the results reveal can mean the difference between life and death.

The doctor will ask you to lie on your back and may put your feet into stirrups. He or she will gently insert an instrument into your vagina to slightly expand its walls. Then what looks like a large cotton bud (or a similar instrument) will be brushed across your cervix to pick up some cells. You may feel a twinge of discomfort. The cells are then sent to a laboratory to be checked for abnormal cell growth, which can lead to cancer. It can take a few weeks to get your result back. However, if you haven't received a result within 6 weeks, contact your doctor. See Gynaecologist.

Cervix After first sex

Cervical smears should become a regular part of a woman's healthcare routine after she turns 20. From time to time, cells in the cervix grow abnormally, usually due to a transient infection with HPV. Mostly these mutant cells go away by themselves, but sometimes they don't. When this happens, you have dysplasia, which means abnormal cell growth. Because dysplasia produces no symptoms, a doctor needs to diagnose it, then treat it as soon as possible. Left untreated, dysplasia can lead to cervical cancer. To be safe, cervical smears are repeated every 3 to 4 years in the United Kingdom (or after 6 months if abnormalities are detected). See Cancer, Cervical Smear, Genital Warts.

↘Cervical smears don't test for vaginal infections, HIV, sexually transmitted infections, or pregnancy. If you want to be tested for these things, tell your doctor.

↘Cervical cancer is highly curable if detected early, which is why routine check-ups make perfect sense.

↘The rate of death from cervical cancer has plummeted since women started having cervical smears 50 years ago.

Chancre

This is a hard, painless sore the size of a small pea that appears in the first stage of syphilis. It shows up between 10 and 90 days after infection in the place where contact was made, usually in or around the genitals, anus, or mouth. Heed this warning sign! A chancre will disappear in a few weeks, but the germs will increase and spread through your body, leading to the nasty complications of syphilis. The bad news is that chancres frequently develop in places where you can't see them, such as inside the anus or on the cervix or the walls of your vagina. This means that many people don't suspect they have syphilis until it's moved on to the second or third stage.

The last thing you want to do is give syphilis to someone else, so if you have a genital ulcer, stop being sexually active until you've had it checked out by a doctor. Be sure to get your partner examined too. Since you often can't tell whether or not someone has a chancre, it's better to practise safer sex until you're certain your partner is syphilis-free. Pronounced SHANK-er. See Safer Sex, Syphilis.

Chlamydia

Everyone should be worried about chlamydia for 2 reasons: it has serious lifelong consequences (infertility, for one) if left untreated, and it's extremely widespread, especially among teenagers. Millions of guys and girls between the ages of 15 and 20 have it, and most of them don't realize it.

Actually, chlamydia is a term that describes a variety of infections caused by a kind of bacteria that live and grow inside the body. The infection that's transmitted sexually—most often through vaginal and anal sex—is called chlamydia trachomatis.

Chlamydia

In females ♀

Frightening but true: up to 80% of females with chlamydia have no symptoms at all. They have a urethra or cervix that's inflamed, but without symptoms, they don't know it. This is dangerous because chlamydia that's left untreated can develop into pelvic inflammatory disease—an infection of the uterus, ovaries, and fallopian tubes that can lead to infertility, or worse, an ectopic pregnancy, which can end in death. Symptoms that do appear in some women include an unusual discharge, a burning sensation when they pee, vaginal bleeding between periods, and abdominal pain. **See Ectopic Pregnancy, Infertility, Pelvic Inflammatory Disease, Testing.**

In males ♂

Watch out: Up to 40% of males with chlamydia have no symptoms at all. Their urethra (water passage) is inflamed, but they have no way of knowing it. Rarely, an infected epididymis (the tiny, very long tube that stores sperm) that goes untreated may lead to infertility. If a guy does have symptoms they will include discomfort when he pees, discharge from his penis, and, if the epididymis is inflamed, pain in the scrotum.

Getting tested
Females ♀

A swab from the cervix, or a urine test, can be done, possibly at the same time as your cervical smear. If you're sexually active and having unprotected sex, you may want to have a test regularly or with each new partner. In some cases chlamydia doesn't show up right away in a test, so if you have reason to believe you've been exposed, get tested again. The results will be returned in 1 to 2 weeks.

Males ♂

The test for chlamydia consists of a doctor or nurse using a swab to remove cells from the opening at the tip of your penis. Some clinics offer a urine test instead of a swab.

Chlamydia
Treatment

After diagnosis, you'll be treated with antibiotics either as a single dose or over several days. This will almost certainly cure you. But a cure doesn't mean you should let down your guard. Having chlamydia once doesn't mean you can't get it again and again, so be careful. While you're undergoing treatment, make sure your partner gets treated too.

Prevention

People with chlamydia look and act normal, which means you can't tell if someone's infected just by looking at them. Given the absence of symptoms, they probably don't even know it themselves! But you can still protect yourself from chlamydia by practising safer sex and by getting tested every 6 months or every time you have a new partner.

Teenagers are more likely to get chlamydia than either syphilis or gonorrhoea.

Q: Who feels more sexual pleasure, guys who are circumcised or guys who are uncircumcised?

A: Because the way we feel sexual pleasure is so personal, no one has an answer to this. However, since there's no difference in erections between circumcised and uncircumcised penises, and no difference in the way a circumcised or uncircumcised penis makes contact with a vagina, there's no physical reason for a difference in sensations.

Q: Is it true that guys who are uncircumcised have a higher chance of becoming infected with HIV?

A: Studies show this is true in the case of male-female sex. Whether you're circumcised or uncircumcised, you can decrease your risk of contracting HIV by wearing a condom.

Circumcision

This is when the foreskin of a penis is removed, usually shortly after birth, for religious or cultural reasons. In some cases adults get circumcised for health reasons. See Foreskin, Smegma.

Cliterectomy
↘female genital mutilation

This is the painful cultural practice of cutting off a young girl's clitoris. A more extreme and agonizing practice is called genital infibulation, where the clitoris is removed and at the same time the 2 labia are scraped away and the vulva is stitched up. When the wounds heal, what's left is a small opening for the passage of urine and menstrual flow. Intercourse only becomes possible when the vulva is cut open for the marriage night, after which it's sewn shut again. A woman in labour has to be opened again to give birth to her child.

There are many reasons cultural groups give for continuing these practices: to maintain family honour; to protect men and newborns from touching the clitoris (which they believe could cause impotence and brain damage); to protect the village from spells; because it's a custom ("we've always done it"); to keep girls "clean"; to make girls more feminine (the clitoris is too much like a penis); and to make sure girls are virgins when they marry. What girls lose in the bargain is the possibility of ever experiencing sexual pleasure and satisfaction. There's also an excellent chance they'll lose their good health.

Following genital infibulation in particular, many girls suffer from a variety of complications for the rest of their lives, including genital malformation and urinary tract infections. Many others die from shock, excessive bleeding, or infection.

Clitoris

↘clit ↘button
↘joy button

The clitoris is the female centre of sexual excitement, and it's much bigger than most people realize. Actually, it's about the same length as the penis, though most of it lies underneath the skin, where you can feel it, but not see it. The part you can see is the small bump of flesh just above the opening to the urethra. This bump, called the head or glans, is protected by a fold of skin called the hood. The head leads under the pubic bone to the long shaft of the clitoris and to the legs, which surround the outside wall of the vagina.

The whole clitoris is extremely sensitive, whether the head is being touched directly with a finger or tongue, or the clitoris legs are being touched indirectly through the walls of the vagina. In fact, the clitoris gets excited in the same way a penis gets excited, by becoming erect. Sometimes the head becomes too sensitive and it feels better to rub the skin around it. Continued gentle stimulation of the clitoris often leads to orgasm.

Clitoridectomy and infibulation are widely performed in most African countries and in several countries in the Middle East and Asia. Over 100 million of the world's female population have undergone one of these "operations," which are usually performed without anaesthetic when a child is between 3 and 6 years old. In the U.K. in the 1800s, clitoridectomy was sometimes performed in an effort to stop women and girls from masturbating, which was considered to be dangerously unhealthy and immoral.

Q&A

Q: How long does it take after infection with the virus for cold sores to show up?

A: They usually appear 2 days to 3 weeks after infection, though it could be longer.

It's easy to become infected with the herpes simplex-1 virus, which causes cold sores in and around the mouth. This virus is very contagious, which means there's a good chance it will enter your body if you kiss someone with cold sores or if you touch their sores with your fingers or another part of your body (such as in oral sex). The virus can also be transmitted by sharing a towel, a toothbrush, or anything else that comes into contact with the sores.

Because there's no cure for herpes simplex-1, most people who have the virus will have recurrent outbreaks of cold sores from time to time for the rest of their lives. Even though outbreaks usually last only a week or 2, for some people they can be the source of considerable distress. For others, having cold sores is no big deal.

Treatment

Once the herpes simplex-1 virus has entered your body, it's there for good. But you can keep outbreaks to a minimum by avoiding stress, eating properly, and getting the rest your body needs. Staying out of the sun also helps. Some doctors may prescribe medication to lessen the frequency of outbreaks.

Prevention

If you have cold sores, wash your hands frequently and avoid sexual contact. Performing oral sex can infect your partner with genital herpes. Or the opposite can happen, where someone who performs oral sex on a person with genital herpes becomes infected around the mouth, leading to cold sores. **See Herpes.**

Communication

You've got to talk to your partner about sex. You probably don't want to (I'm too shy! I'm embarrassed! I'm afraid!) but you've got to screw up your courage and speak your mind anyway. The reason is simple: you deserve to have your needs met in your relationship. If your partner isn't interested in hearing what you have to say, then it's time to find someone new. If you're in a relationship where you both care a lot about each other, then it won't be so hard. After all, your partner isn't telepathic, and can only know what's on your mind if you speak up.

The first step in good communication is to know your own feelings. The second step is to respect them. For example, if someone wants to have sex with you but you've decided you won't go that far, stick to your decision. Girls especially have a tendency to worry too much about hurting their partner's feelings. As a result, they end up doing things that make them feel bad. Saying what's on your mind doesn't mean you have to be rude or cruel. Just honest and kind, or funny, if possible.

Things to talk about

⬎ Birth control and what you'll do if pregnancy occurs.
⬎ Protection, because no one wants to become infected with HIV or herpes or whatever else is out there.
⬎ Which kinds of sexual activities you're ready to try, and which kinds you'd rather hold off on.
⬎ Where you like to be touched and other things that make you feel good. Just because you're in love—or lust—it doesn't mean your partner magically knows what turns you on.
⬎ What you don't like. If you keep pretending to love the way your partner kisses you or rubs your privates when it's really a big turn-off, your frustration will grow, not your love.

♀ Q & A

Q: My boyfriend wants to put his fingers in my vagina, but I don't want him to. What should I do?

A: It's up to you to tell him clearly what you don't want. If he keeps trying, it means he doesn't believe you or he doesn't care. Either way, you should look for a new boyfriend. You want someone you can talk to about your limits and who will respect them and like you anyway.

There's no formula for saying the right thing at the right time. You just have to brave it. If something is bothering you, silence = disaster.

Q: Can I get pregnant if I don't have an orgasm?

A: Absolutely. Once sperm are in your body, they head immediately to the fallopian tubes, whether or not you've climaxed.

Q: Can a girl get pregnant during her period?

A: Yes. It's possible, though rare, to ovulate during your period, which means it's possible to get pregnant.

Q: Will douching after sex stop conception?

A: No such luck. No matter what kind of liquid you inject into your vagina after sex, the sperm will already be on their way to the fallopian tubes. It only takes a few seconds for sperm to swim through the cervix. Once they're in the uterus, they're home free. As for douching, it's usually a bad idea. See Douching.

Q: Is it possible to get pregnant if you have sex in the bath or in a pool?

A: Yes. Making love underwater doesn't prevent sperm from racing to find an egg to fertilize.

Q: Can I get pregnant if my boyfriend ejaculates into the bath water?

A: No. Most of the sperm will die, and the ones that don't will have a tough time finding the opening to your vagina.

Conception

When semen is ejaculated near or inside the vagina around the time of ovulation, conception becomes a possibility. Conception is the moment when a male sperm unites with a female egg, almost always in one of the fallopian tubes. The egg is now fertilized and is called a zygote. When the zygote settles into the wall of the uterus about 2 weeks later, pregnancy has begun.

Ovulation usually takes place 2 weeks after the first day of menstruation, though some girls ovulate earlier or later. Because sperm can live for up to a week in the body and an egg can live for 2 days, conception generally happens 7 to 16 days after menstruation starts. However, ovulation can be irregular for a variety of reasons, which means there are no "safe days" in the cycle to have unprotected sex. See Birth Control, Emergency Contraception, Ovulation, Pregnancy, Sexual Intercourse.

Condoms

↘rubbers ↘johnnies
↘prophylactics
↘love gloves

It's no mystery why condoms are so popular. For a low price they allow people to have an active sex life without worrying too much about pregnancy. They also offer excellent protection against HIV and several other sexually transmitted infections. As birth control, condoms work by stopping the sperm from entering the vagina. As protection against STIs, they work by blocking the exchange of fluids between partners and by reducing skin-to-skin contact. Unfortunately, condoms protect less effectively against herpes, genital warts, syphilis, molluscum contagiosum, and pubic lice, which can be spread from other areas of the skin besides the penis and vagina.

Male condoms ♂

Condoms are very thin latex sheaths made in the shape of an erect penis, then rolled up and packaged in a small plastic wrapper or container. For better protection against both pregnancy and STIs, you can also buy condoms that are shaped to hold the testicles, though these might be hard to find. Men who are sensitive or allergic to latex can purchase polyurethane condoms. Condoms made of sheep membrane are also available, but they only protect against pregnancy, not HIV or STIs (viruses and bacteria can pass through the membrane). You'll know you have a problem with latex if the skin on your penis becomes dry or itchy, or if a rash or welts appear.

Usually one size fits all, but if you're concerned that you're too small or too large for a regular condom, some brands make them in small, medium, and large. Other choices include dry or lubricated, and with spermicide or without. Only buy condoms

♂ How to use them

Condoms are 88% effective in preventing pregnancy. If you use a spermicide every time you have sex, you can increase the effectiveness to 97%. And if you carefully follow this list, you will greatly reduce your risk of catching an STI. But before you get started, check the expiry date. If the condom is old, throw it away.

1. Put the condom on when your penis is erect, not before.
2. Open the package carefully, making sure you don't cut or tear the condom in the process. If you know you're going to have sex, open the package ahead of time to save a few seconds, but don't take the condom out.
3. Take out the condom and place it over the tip of your penis. Squeeze the air out of the reservoir. If there's no reservoir, pinch the end to make a place for the sperm to go. This is the moment to pull back your foreskin if you're uncircumcised.
4. Unroll the condom all the way to the base of your penis.
5. Smooth out the condom to get rid of air bubbles.
6. As soon as you ejaculate, take your penis out of your partner's vagina, anus, or mouth (if you're still in when you get soft, semen can spill out the top). Make sure you hold the base of the condom while you're pulling out.
7. Still holding the base, slip your penis out of the condom and throw the condom away.

Male Condoms

that have a reservoir at the end to catch the semen. The reservoir lowers the risk of the condom breaking when you ejaculate. Heat weakens condoms, so never leave them in the sun or in the glove compartment of your car. Last but not least, only use water-based lubricants with your condom. Latex that comes into contact with oil-based products, such as hand lotion, Vaseline, suntan lotion, and cooking oils, will begin to deteriorate in 30 seconds.

Some people groan at the mention of the word condom. It's true that condoms can be a hassle, but they're a lot better than the consequences (infections, disease, unintended pregnancy). Try making them part of your sex play. Get your girlfriend or boyfriend to put it on just the way you like it. But first, drop a bit of water-based lubricant into the end to increase your pleasure (not too much or the condom may slip off). Or check out some of the shapes and textures that are on the market. If you can't find something you can have fun with, you're not using your imagination. Make sure you read the packages of novelty condoms carefully because some are designed only to spice up your sex life, not to provide protection.

Advantages

Offers very good protection against almost everything. Can delay ejaculation. Easy to get and inexpensive. Can be slipped into a pocket or small purse for ready portability. Available in a variety of colours, shapes, textures, and flavours. Sex still feels good for most guys and girls.

Disadvantages

Doesn't fully protect against STIs (herpes, genital warts, syphilis, chancroid, molluscum contagiosum, and crabs) that can be contracted from uncovered areas of skin. Incorrect usage can lead to pregnancy. Can slip off or break during use. If made from latex, can cause an allergic reaction in some people. Can put a dent in spontaneous sex. Reduces feelings of pleasure during intercourse for many guys and girls. Cuts down on the fun of oral sex for anyone who doesn't like the taste of latex (using an edible lubricant may help). Demands action as soon as you ejaculate (you have to remove it, which means you can't automatically relax into the arms of your lover). A tiny percentage are defective.

Availability

Most chemists carry a good variety of condoms. Some larger stores also carry polyurethane condoms and ones made from sheep membrane. The Internet offers a huge selection, but at some sites you have to be of legal age to make a purchase. Condoms are also available at supermarkets and petrol stations. When you're old enough to go to clubs and bars, they can be bought from vending machines in the toilets.

Q & A

Q: What if a guy says he's too big to wear a condom?

A: Unless he's enormous, most condoms will fit just fine. If he is enormous, several brands make large-size condoms.

Female condoms ♀

Female condoms do the same thing as male condoms—they protect against pregnancy and sexually transmitted infections, including HIV. Made of a thin, soft plastic, these condoms are shaped to fit comfortably inside the vagina. They can be put in up to 8 hours before sex, and left in for up to 8 hours afterwards as long as the woman remains lying down (if you get up before removing the condom, semen will spill out the end). Because of its close fit, the female condom can be used in a variety of sexual positions.

Available in the U.K. since 1992, the female condom is an excellent but not very well known alternative to the male condom. Imagine a large, loose male condom with a ring at both ends. That's a female condom. The ring at the closed end is soft and flexible and is used to insert the condom and keep it securely in place. The ring at the open end (where the penis enters) is also soft and flexible. It hangs about 1 inch outside the vagina, partially covering the vaginal lips. Female condoms come in 1 size only and are already partly filled with lubrication. More lube is frequently needed to keep the lovemaking friction-free. At the time of writing, there are no flavoured or textured female condoms on the market. Female condoms can only be used once before being thrown away.

The most important thing to know about the female condom is that at first it can be hard to put in. With practice, putting it in usually gets easier. But do all your practising before actually using it as protection. A female condom that's put in poorly may not protect you from pregnancy and infection. You also won't be protected if it's not used correctly, which means you need the cooperation of your partner. He has to be unperturbed by the look (some people find it strange-looking), and willing to have you guide his penis into the entrance. He also has to be ready to stop if his penis, by accident, slides down the side of the condom into your vagina. Another reason to stop is if his thrusting pulls the condom out of your vagina or pushes the outside ring into it (if this happens, more lube is needed, either inside the condom or straight onto his penis). A female condom and a male condom can't be used at the same time.

How to use them

When used correctly, female condoms are effective about 95% of the time at preventing pregnancy. Because they cover more skin than the male condom does, they offer even better protection against some STIs such as herpes and genital warts. When you're putting one in, prepare to be patient, because with all that lubrication the condom is bound to be slippery.

1. As you open the package, make sure you don't cut or tear the condom.
2. Rub the condom between your fingers to spread the lubrication evenly around the inside. If you want to add lubricant, this is the best time to do it.
3. Make sure the inside ring is at the closed end.
4. Find a comfortable position (standing, sitting, or squatting), with your knees apart.
5. Hold the condom at the closed end between your thumb and middle finger. The open end will be hanging down.
6. Squeeze the closed end between your thumb and middle finger, keeping your index finger free so it can be ready for step 8.
7. This is the part where you have to be patient. With your other hand, spread open your vaginal lips and insert the condom into your vagina. If it slips, try again. Make sure it goes in straight.
8. Using the index finger of the hand holding the condom, push the condom in as far as it will go.
9. Use your hand to guide your boyfriend's penis into your vagina.
10. After your lovemaking and before you stand up, remove the condom. Make sure you squeeze the outer ring shut to keep the semen from spilling. Throw the condom in the bin.

Q: Can I use a female condom if I have my period?

A: Yes, but put it in just before having sex.

Q: What if I'm wearing a female condom and I have to pee?

A: There's no problem. Urine comes out the urethra, which is just above the vagina. All you have to do is move the outer ring to one side.

Q: Why do guys think girls who carry condoms with them are too into sex?

A: We live in a society that discriminates against girls who are sexually aware or active. Guys express this discrimination by calling these girls sluts and whores. It's ironic that girls who show the same interest in sex that many guys do are put down for it by those very same guys. If this happens to you, do your best to ignore the insults. Being prepared is common sense. See Double Standard.

Female Condoms

Advantages

Gives women control over their own protection, not only against pregnancy, but also against HIV and other sexually transmitted infections. Available without a physical examination or prescription. Made of polyurethane, not latex, which makes it an alternative for people who are allergic to latex. Can be used with water-based and oil-based lubricants. Warms immediately to body temperature. Fits the contours of the vagina. Stronger than latex, therefore less likely to break than a male condom. Easy to carry. Many women and men say sex feels better than with a male condom.

Disadvantages

Doesn't fully protect against herpes, genital warts, syphilis, molluscum contagiosum, and crabs. Can be pulled out of place if there's not enough lubrication. Can be difficult to put in at first. Can break or be defective. More expensive than a male condom. Boyfriend's cooperation is needed. Some women find it uncomfortable. Others say it makes a noise (embarrassing for some people, amusing for others). The penis can slip down the side of the condom by mistake, risking pregnancy. Pregnancy can also result if the outer ring gets pushed inside the vagina during thrusting.

Availability

The only brand of female condom on the market is called Femidom. It can be found in pharmacies and where other forms of protection are sold, or it can be ordered over the Internet.

No condom = no sex.

For near-perfect protection against pregnancy and sexually transmitted infections, use condoms with the Pill. Condoms and foam together also provide excellent protection.

Confidentiality

For a variety of reasons, some teenagers prefer to keep the details of their sexual health separate from their relationship with their parents. If you choose to see a doctor or health care provider by yourself, perhaps without your parents' knowledge, they have a duty to keep all information about you confidential —whatever your age. Confidentiality is when you can discuss medical or sexual issues with your doctor without the involvement of your parents or anyone else. In other words, whatever goes on in the doctor's office is your own business.

Even though the age of consent for hetero-sexual intercourse is 16 in Great Britain and 17 in Northern Ireland, doctors may prescribe contra-ception to people under this age if they feel they are competent to understand the issues involved. See Parental Consent.

Consensual Sex

According to the law, any kind of sex must be con-sensual, which means that both partners must agree to it. This is true whether the couple is planning on kissing, having sexual intercourse, sharing sexual fantasies, or doing anything else that's sexually intimate. Consensual sex doesn't mean getting a "yes" after putting pressure on someone; nor does it mean assuming a yes if someone isn't clear about saying no. It means knowing that your partner is comfortable and willing because he or she has said so, freely and clearly. See Rape, Sexual Assault.

Cunnilingus

STIs you can get

- HIV
- herpes
- syphilis
- gonorrhoea
- hepatitis B
- genital warts

Cunnilingus
↘ eating out
↘ going down
↘ muff diving

This kind of lovemaking involves using your lips or tongue to give pleasure to a woman's clitoris and surrounding area. Because cunnilingus directly but softly stimulates the clitoris, for many women orgasm is reached much more easily this way than by intercourse.

Protection

If you're the one giving cunnilingus and you're not sure your partner is free of HIV and other sexually transmitted infections, it's smart to use protection. If she's infected with syphilis, herpes, or hepatitis B, you could easily catch it. If she has HIV, there's a small chance you could contract it from her vaginal fluids, and the risk increases if she has her period. There's a much smaller chance of catching gonorrhoea. If you're the one getting "eaten," you're also at risk of catching herpes, syphilis, hepatitis B and, uncommonly, gonorrhoea. Genital warts may occasionally be transferred to guys via oral sex.

The recommended protection during cunnilingus is to place a dam over the vulva, though even a dam might not protect you from herpes and genital warts (you could pick these up by touching skin that isn't covered by the dam). While it's true that dams can be a drag on the romance and excitement of the moment, they can save you a lot of trouble later on. One way to make it more enjoyable for your partner is to put lubricant on the side of the dam that touches her skin. **See Dam, Oral Sex.**

Cybersex

↳on-line sex

Internet chat rooms are busy. Every day men and women of all ages and sexual orientations log on to form on-line sexual relationships with strangers. For the most part, people share their erotic fantasies. Some flirt. Others masturbate while "talking" on-screen. One of the things people like about expressing themselves sexually over the computer is the anonymity it offers. No one knows who you are. Even better, virtual sex is safe: no sexually transmitted infections, no pregnancy, no broken hearts. But there's no actual relationship, either, which is why many people who try cybersex quickly lose interest.

Cybersex only gets risky when you "fall in love" with someone on-screen and suddenly find yourself involved in a cyber romance. But who exactly is this new love of your life? The truth is, you have no idea. Lying online is very common. People lie about their age, their appearance, and even their interests for all sorts of reasons: for the fun of it, because they're insecure, because they have something to hide, because they're crazy. Considering how dangerous some people can be, it's smart not to give out any personal information, including your full name, address, and phone number. If you're determined to meet your cyber sweetheart, arrange to take a friend with you and meet in a public place. This way, you can easily get away if you have to. Make sure someone knows where you're going and when you'll be home.

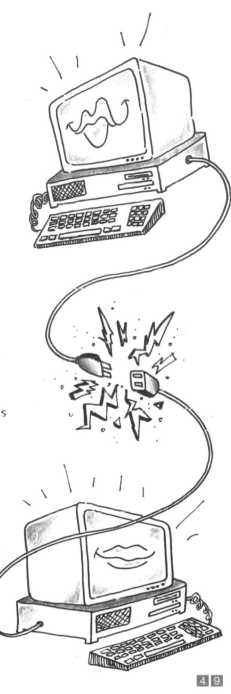

Cystitis

⬎urinary tract infection
⬎bladder infection

You have cystitis if the inner lining of your bladder is inflamed, usually due to infection. Symptoms include a burning sensation or pain when you pee, pressure on your pelvis, feeling like you have to pee all the time even though you just went, smelly or cloudy urine, lower-back pain, and fever. A small amount of blood in the urine is also common.

The most common cause of cystitis is when bacteria that normally live in the bowel get pushed into the urethra. The bacteria travel through the urethra to the bladder, which then becomes infected. Usually, it's females who get cystitis because the opening to their urethra is so close to the vagina and anus. During sexual activity it's easy for germs to be carried on their partner's fingertips or penis, or on their own fingers, from one of these locations to the urethra. Also, a woman's urethra is only about an inch and a half long, which means germs don't have far to go before they reach the bladder. Rarely, men also develop cystitis.

Treatment

At the first sign of cystitis, increase your fluid intake and make an appointment to see your doctor. While you're waiting for your appointment, drink plenty of cranberry juice, preferably unsweetened (the less sugar, the more actual juice). The juice will make your urine more acidic, which will slow the growth of the bacteria, and will also stop the bacteria from sticking to the lining of your bladder. At the doctor's office, a sample of your urine will be examined for bacteria. If you have cystitis, your doctor will prescribe antibiotics. If the symptoms persist even after you've finished the antibiotics, ask if you can be tested again to determine exactly which bacteria are causing the infection. Although bladder infections are usually treated successfully, they can be very serious if the infection spreads to the kidneys. If you suffer repeated bouts of cystitis, your doctor may want to run further tests to see if there's an underlying cause.

Prevention

After going to the bathroom, always wipe from front to back. Also, urinate as soon as possible after having sex to clear your urethra (it's easy for bacteria to get pushed into the opening of the urethra during foreplay and intercourse). Drinking lots of fluids, particularly cranberry juice, and peeing frequently will also help keep your urethra clear.

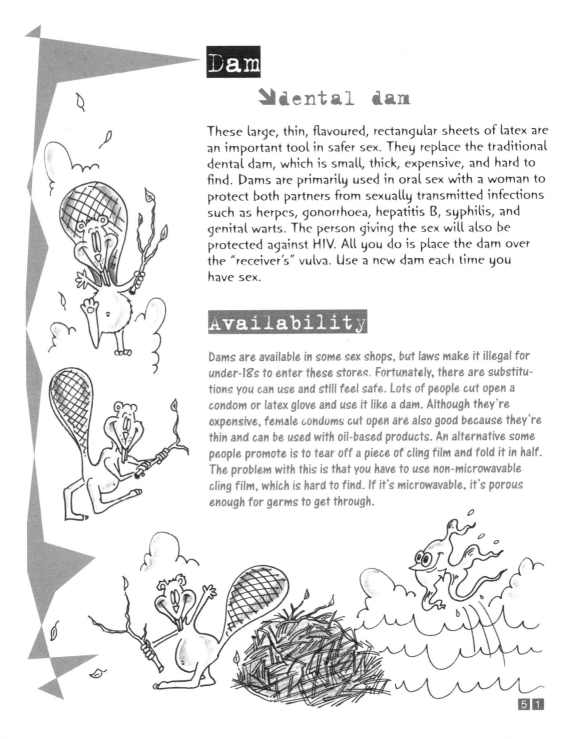

Dam

↳dental dam

These large, thin, flavoured, rectangular sheets of latex are an important tool in safer sex. They replace the traditional dental dam, which is small, thick, expensive, and hard to find. Dams are primarily used in oral sex with a woman to protect both partners from sexually transmitted infections such as herpes, gonorrhoea, hepatitis B, syphilis, and genital warts. The person giving the sex will also be protected against HIV. All you do is place the dam over the "receiver's" vulva. Use a new dam each time you have sex.

Availability

Dams are available in some sex shops, but laws make it illegal for under-18s to enter these stores. Fortunately, there are substitutions you can use and still feel safe. Lots of people cut open a condom or latex glove and use it like a dam. Although they're expensive, female condoms cut open are also good because they're thin and can be used with oil-based products. An alternative some people promote is to tear off a piece of cling film and fold it in half. The problem with this is that you have to use non-microwavable cling film, which is hard to find. If it's microwavable, it's porous enough for germs to get through.

Depo-Provera ♀

This is a method to avoid pregnancy that involves getting an injection 4 times a year. You start by making an appointment to see a doctor during the first few days of your period. At the appointment you're given an injection of a synthetic hormone, progesterone, which affects the body in 3 ways: it stops ovulation; it makes the uterus uninviting to an egg if one is released by mistake; and it thickens the mucus that blocks the cervix, making it harder for sperm to swim through. After the appointment you go home and carry on with your life, though now there's a 99.9% chance you won't get pregnant (beginning a week after the injection). Unfortunately, you won't be protected at all from sexually transmitted infections, which means you or your partner still need to use a condom. Every 12 weeks you return for another shot, in either your thigh, upper arm, or buttocks.

Availability

Though first introduced in 1974, Depo-Provera has only been widely available since 1994. It is now offered as a contraception option at all family planning clinics.

Advantages

Is extremely easy to use. Is ideal for women who find it hard to remember to take the Pill every day. Can be taken by people who are sensitive to oestrogen. Periods are lighter and actually disappear in 50% of the women who use it (this might not seem like a good thing to some women). Can be taken by women of all ages, as well as by breastfeeding mothers. Has all the advantages of the birth control pill.

Disadvantages

Doesn't protect against any sexually transmitted infections. May cause unpredictable spotting or bleeding in the first few months. Can cause an increase in appetite. Women who want to have a child may have to wait up to 18 months from the time of their last injection before their body can conceive.

Desire

↘libido   ↘sex drive
↘lust   ↘horniness

Desire is the urge to have sex. Experts say it begins in the brain, though if you're a guy you may argue it begins in the body, front and centre, many times a day! But not all guys are non-stop horny. The truth is, libido is as individual as body hair. Some people have a lot of it, others have only a tiny bit, and everyone else is in between.

The strength of your desire is never a problem in itself. It only becomes a problem if you're in a relationship with someone whose desire is drastically different from yours. Also, your libido may change throughout your life depending on your age, fitness level, how you feel about yourself, the quality of your relationship with your partner, and what's going on in your life in general.

Feelings of attraction and desire are natural and begin in both sexes around puberty. Unfortunately, taboos about sex make it uncomfortable for many teenagers to openly explore their feelings as they become aware of them. Many people, especially heterosexual women, lesbians, and gay men, live their entire lives without fully acknowledging their feelings of desire. In fact, the world has a long history of discouraging expressions of sexual desire in these groups, as well as in individuals whose sexual orientation is less readily defined, such as bisexuals and transvestites. Throughout history, male heterosexual desire has generally been accepted and indulged.

Desire

In females

Many women of all ages are in the habit of denying their feelings of sexual desire. As a result, they can't express them. Instead, they make themselves attractive so others will desire them. Girls who fall into this group often worry more about satisfying their partner's desire than understanding and satisfying their own. On the contrary, girls who are comfortable with their feelings and who express them risk being called sluts, even if they don't actually have sex with anyone. According to the stereotype, "good girls" aren't interested in sex, only "bad girls" are. This is slowly changing in the United Kingdom, where an increasing number of girls are aware of their feelings and are comfortable with them. Their awareness and comfort gives these girls a positive edge when it comes to making decisions about sex. **See Double Standard.**

In males

Guys have a reputation of being predators, of always feeling desire and being willing to do just about anything to appease it. While many guys fit this stereotype, there are lots who don't. Some guys are more interested in sports or academic studies than scoring with girls. For other guys, the priority is to build a caring, intimate relationship, and sex comes later. Others lack confidence in their sexuality, or have a low level of desire, or feel shy, or don't think they're attractive. There are also plenty of guys who don't want to have sex until marriage for religious or personal reasons. All of these guys end up battling other people's preconceptions of them. When it comes to "taking action," there are many guys who don't feel up to it. Taking the initiative in sexual relationships is nerve-wracking, and plenty of guys are happy when the roles reverse (girl meets guy, girl asks guy out, and so on).

Q & A

Q: Are hairy guys more sex-crazed than smooth-bodied ones?

A: A guy's desire for sex has nothing to do with body hair. It has to do with his openness to sex and how much testosterone is circulating in his body. How much hair a guy has is determined by the genes he inherited from his parents.

Q: What's the difference between love and lust?

A: Loving someone means loving the whole person sexually and romantically. You enjoy that person's company and are interested in what they're doing and thinking, and you want that person to be happy. Feeling lust for someone means feeling intense desire for his or her body. Your interest focuses on the sexual pleasure you can get from being together.

Diaphragm ♀

This method of birth control prevents sperm from entering the uterus by blocking the cervix. Made of latex and shaped like a shallow bowl, the diaphragm fits comfortably over your cervix when inserted properly. You shouldn't even feel it, and neither should your partner. This is a good choice of birth control if you only have sex occasionally.

A doctor will examine you and give you a prescription for the right size. When you return with the diaphragm, the doctor will show you how to use it. Later, at home, practise putting the diaphragm in. Fold it in half and slip it face up into your vagina. When you let go, it will open up and cover your cervix. Leave it in for several hours to see if it's comfortable. If it causes lower back or abdominal pain, it's probably too big. To take it out, hook the rim of the diaphragm with your finger and pull. It's important to practise so that when it's time to rely on your diaphragm, you'll know you can put it in right. The first time you use it, your partner should wear a condom in case there are any problems and you have to take it out.

To be just over 90% effective, the diaphragm must be used with a spermicide (put 2 to 3 teaspoons into the "bowl" just before insertion), and new spermicide must be added to your vagina each time you have sex. It can be inserted up to 6 hours before intercourse and must be left in place for at least 6 hours afterwards, but not longer than 24 hours. If you put the diaphragm in early you need to add more spermicide just before sex.

If you take care of your diaphragm— wash it with mild soap and water after use,

Diaphragm

dry it thoroughly, sprinkle it with a bit of cornflour to absorb humidity, and store it in a safe place—it should last 1 to 2 years. To be sure it's in good shape, check it every once in a while for weak spots or holes by holding it up to the light or filling it with water. Drops that form on the underside indicate a hole. Women who gain or lose 5kg or more need to be fitted with a new diaphragm.

Advantages

Doesn't cause hormonal changes to the body. In most women there are no side effects. Offers some protection from chlamydia and gonorrhoea. Can be used during menstruation. Can be inserted early so as not to interrupt sex play. Is inexpensive and easy to care for. Can help you become familiar with your body.

Disadvantages

Can be hard to put in. Failure rates are higher in teenagers, who may not be as motivated to put it in correctly. Can be dislodged during sex, especially if the woman is on top. Must be used with a spermicide, which can be messy and can irritate the skin of either partner. Doesn't offer protection from HIV and several other sexually transmitted infections. Spontaneous sex must be interrupted to put the diaphragm in (though you can turn this into a fun part of your play). Some women are allergic to latex. Rarely, may cause urinary tract infections.

Availability

To be fitted with a diaphragm you need to make an appointment with your doctor, or family planning clinic. Don't leave the doctor's office until you've practised putting it in and taking it out. Diaphragms, like most other forms of contraception, are available free of charge in the United Kingdom if you obtain a prescription from your doctor.

Q: If you use a dildo, does that mean you're messed up sexually?

A: There's nothing wrong with using a dildo. Enjoying sexual pleasure is an important and healthy part of adult life. Dildos are toys for when you feel like playing.

Using a dildo won't stretch your vagina or change its shape in any way.

Dildos

These sex toys have been around for centuries. Like their ancient counterparts, modern-day dildos are used to bring pleasure to the vagina and anus, usually by penetration. Available in a variety of sizes, many dildos are made to look like an erect penis, though some are shaped in more whimsical forms such as a banana or a porpoise. The latter are often preferred by lesbians who find the penis shape unexciting.

People who enjoy dildos usually have their own, but if you happen to be sharing, use it with a condom, and before giving it to your partner, change the condom. This is necessary because some dildos absorb body fluids, which means they can transmit HIV (though the chance of this is very small). If your sex play takes you from the anus to the vagina, change the condom to avoid bacterial infection.

If you don't have condoms on hand, all sex toys should be disinfected before being shared. The best dildos for sharing are the silicone kind because they're non-porous and can be sterilized by boiling them in water for 3 to 4 minutes. This will kill all bacteria. Plastic dildos can't be boiled, but can be disinfected by washing them with a solution of 10 parts water to 1 part bleach. Then rinse and dry thoroughly. Dildos aren't the same as vibrators, which are used primarily for stimulation. See Vibrators.

Doctors

It's great if you like and trust your family doctor. But what if you don't? What if you're thinking of becoming sexually active and you discover you can't be open with the doctor you've been going to since childhood? You have 2 choices, find a new doctor (ask your friends or parents for recommendations, or look in the Yellow Pages) or see a doctor or nurse at a family planning, GU medicine or social health clinic. Avoiding doctors is not an option.

When dealing with doctors, nurses, and other health care providers, you need to be able to ask the questions that are important to you. Before your appointment, make sure you know what those questions are. Then expect frank answers. If you feel you're not being taken seriously or you're being disrespected in any way, look elsewhere for health care, but don't give up. If you're sexually active, you need information about sexually transmitted infections, and if you're having sexual intercourse, you need birth control. Eventually, you may also need a place to go for STI testing. If you're having sex with numerous partners, getting tested must become a routine part of your health care.
See Cervical Smear, Confidentiality, Gynaecologist, Testing.

Double Standard

This is when the same behaviour is viewed differently depending on whether you belong to one group or another. For example, in traditional views, girls who have sex with several guys are considered to be easy and cheap, while guys who sleep with lots of girls are considered to be skilful, powerful, and more masculine. Despite the fact that many people still hold traditional views, double standards don't carry as much weight as they once did. These days, fewer people believe that girls should hold on to their virginity until marriage while guys should "sow their wild oats".

Q & A

Q: What does it mean when a doctor asks if you're sexually active?

A: Usually, the doctor is asking if you're having sexual intercourse. He or she wants to know if you need birth control or information about sexually transmitted infections. Because STIs can also be transmitted through oral sex, anal sex, and mutual masturbation, if you're doing any of these, you should tell your doctor.

Q & A

Q: Why do girls have to shave the hair on their legs, armpits, and bikini line to be beautiful, when guys can be beautiful without shaving—even though they're hairier than us?

A: Girls don't have to remove their body hair to be beautiful, they just think they do. Decades of advertising has convinced grandmothers, their daughters, and their daughters' daughters that smooth, hairless bodies are not only the ultimate in beauty, but very hygienic too. It doesn't help that most men also believe this. Interestingly, hundreds of years of literature and art have produced many thousands of strikingly beautiful women, all of whom were hairy. Unfortunately, recent advertising has started to target guys as well, suggesting that only hairless male bodies are beautiful and sexy.

Douching ♀

If no one ever douched again, it would be a good thing. Douching means washing out your vagina with warm water or a shop-bought solution. This requires a special bag or bottle that shoots the liquid up your vagina. In days gone by, some women douched because they disliked their vaginal odour and were afraid others would notice it and be turned off (on the contrary, many men and women are aroused by the female sex smell). Other women did it because they thought it was a normal part of hygiene. Now we know that douching is unhealthy because it washes away the fluids in the vagina that naturally keep it clean. Without these fluids, the vagina can easily become infected. Some douches even damage the vaginal lining, making it more vulnerable to infection. Perfumed douches are particularly bad because they may cause irritation or an allergic reaction. Although douching is not generally encouraged, it is sometimes recommended for women with excessive vaginal secretions for which no infective cause can be found.

As birth control

Douching won't do anything to prevent pregnancy, no matter how soon you douche after intercourse. It takes sperm only a few minutes to reach the cervix, then they're in and on their way to the fallopian tubes, where conception usually takes place. Douching may even propel the sperm toward the cervix faster.

Drugs

⬊amphetamines ⬊speed

⬊barbiturates ⬊downers

⬊cannabis ⬊marijuana

⬊pot ⬊hash ⬊acid

⬊cocaine ⬊coke ⬊crack

⬊ecstasy ⬊heroin

⬊junk ⬊smack

⬊psilocybin mushrooms

⬊magic mushrooms

⬊shrooms ⬊angel dust

⬊tobacco ⬊cigarettes

⬊smokes

All drugs, whether they're highly addictive or not, or very dangerous or not, can have a negative effect on your sex life. For example, getting high can lead you to do sexual things you wouldn't normally do with people you wouldn't be caught dead with on any other day. Afterwards, you may feel bad about it, or angry or scared, depending on what happened and who your partner was. But mixing drugs with sex can cause more than bad feelings. If no one bothers with protection (when you're high, protection can seem irrelevant), pregnancy can result, or infection with HIV or other sexually transmitted infections. Also, someone who is too spaced out to fight back makes an easy target for sexual assault.

Like alcohol, drugs can make you feel horny. But this effect doesn't last. Habitual use of amphetamines and barbiturates can affect sexual performance in both males and females: guys find it harder to get and keep an erection, and women have trouble lubricating. It can also make having an orgasm a thing of the past. The same things can happen to people who take cocaine, with the added problem in some users of having their sexual desire destroyed completely. Sexual desire is also weakened in many people who smoke a large amount of cannabis. Last but not least, tobacco constricts the small blood vessels in the penis. As a result, in some smokers erections are less frequent and don't last as long as they might otherwise.

Q & A

Q: Can sperm get through clothes?

A: If the guy comes and he's wearing clothes and you are too, you have nothing to worry about.

Dry Sex

↘ **body rubbing**

↘ **outercourse**

↘ **dry humping**

↘ **frottage**

Basically, dry sex is doing everything you'd normally do with a partner when you're both turned on and ready to go—touching, kissing, masturbating each other—but with your clothes on. The great advantage of dry sex is that there's no skin contact at the genitals level, which means that nothing bad can come from it: no HIV, no sexually transmitted infections, no pregnancy. If both partners agree that dry sex is their limit, it can be fun, intimate, and satisfying.

For some people, dry sex means doing all of the above, but with both partners naked. In this case, it's important to be certain that your partner understands and is willing to respect your limits. You don't want to find yourself in a situation where one minute you're playing and having fun, and the next minute you're being sexually assaulted.

Protection

If you've got your clothes on, no protection is needed. If nakedness is involved, you have to think about protecting yourself from the kinds of STIs you can get from touching someone else's skin, such as herpes and genital warts. **See Safer Sex.**

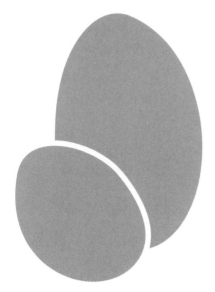

Ectopic Pregnancy ♀

↘tubal pregnancy

In a normal pregnancy, the fertilized egg spends a few days in the fallopian tube before heading over to the uterus, where it will develop into an embryo. In an ectopic pregnancy, the egg gets trapped in the fallopian tube and starts to develop there. Symptoms that this has happened include bleeding from the vagina and severe pain in the lower abdomen. You may also feel pain in your chest or shoulder. You must immediately go to a hospital to have the embryo surgically removed. If you don't, the tube will eventually burst, causing internal bleeding that can be fatal. Women with pelvic inflammatory disease have a higher risk of developing an ectopic pregnancy. See Pelvic Inflammatory Disease.

Eggs

↘ova

About 9 months after an egg and a sperm unite, a baby is born. If this newborn is female, she has up to 400,000 female sex cells in her 2 tiny ovaries. These cells are actually immature eggs. Every month after puberty, one of these eggs matures and is released from an ovary. It's then drawn into the nearest fallopian tube. As it moves down the tube on its way to the uterus, it may or may not be fertilized by a sperm. If it isn't fertilized, the egg disintegrates and leaves the body through the vagina as part of the normal vaginal discharge. Between puberty and menopause, up to 500 sex cells mature into eggs and are released. See Ovulation.

Ejaculation ♂

↘coming ↘creaming
↘climaxing
↘shooting your load
↘blowing your wad

This is when semen shoots out the tip of an erect penis in a quick series of squirts. Orgasm usually occurs at the same time, though climaxing and ejaculating aren't always simultaneous. Actually, it's possible to ejaculate and not climax. When this happens, it can be a letdown.

Ejaculation is almost always the result of being sexually stimulated, either by a partner or by masturbating. But it's also normal to ejaculate at night during sleep as part of a sexy dream, or sometimes for no reason at all. Many guys get one or more erections over the course of a night, though most don't end in ejaculation. From the very first time a guy ejaculates, he can get a girl pregnant. See Wet Dreams.

Premature ejaculation

No matter what kind of sex you're having, there's no standard time for ejaculating. It can happen right after penetration, or even at the touch of a hand. In heterosexual sex, more experienced guys are able to thrust for several minutes, and some seem to be able to go on forever. If you and your partner are satisfied with the amount of time it takes you to ejaculate, then there's no problem. But if you come before you want to, or before your partner wants you to, you might feel frustrated.

The easiest way to gain control of your timing is to practise "holding off" when you masturbate. Bring yourself

Q & A

Q : What if a guy comes before he even gets his pants off?

A : If he's still excited, another erection will come along in 10 or 20 minutes. You can use the intervening time to enjoy each other's bodies.

Ejaculation

In females

It can happen that a small amount of clear fluid shoots out the urethra during sexual stimulation, either before or after orgasm. Many people think this fluid is urine, but it isn't. It's called female ejaculate, and researchers are still trying to understand what it is and where it comes from. Many women never experience this phenomenon. If you ejaculate during sex, you may be surprised, but there's no reason to be embarrassed. Female ejaculation is just another way the body functions.

close to ejaculation, then stop. Do this several times before you allow yourself to come. You can also practise with a partner, either by mutual masturbation or penetration. The more you practise holding off, the sooner you'll gain the control you want. Being relaxed also helps. If your buttocks, abdomen, and thighs are clenched, you'll come faster.

Another way to delay ejaculation when you're about to come is to hold your penis at the base and squeeze. Or your partner can hold it. Squeezing the other end of the penis just under the head will have the same effect. Wearing a condom can also help you hold on to your arousal longer. Finally, frequent masturbation may desensitize your penis, with the result that you won't come the minute it's touched, but this doesn't work for everyone.

Retarded ejaculation

If you have an erection and you're really excited and your penis continues to be stimulated but you can't ejaculate, or it takes a very, very long time (over half an hour), you may have a problem called retarded ejaculation. This has nothing to do with IQ. It could be that you've drunk too much alcohol. Or you could have a strong underlying fear of something to do with ejaculation, such as getting your girlfriend pregnant. If you think you have this condition, it might help to see a sex therapist who is trained in helping people overcome problems like this one.

Retrograde ejaculation

Normally semen is propelled through the urethra and out the tip of the penis. Occasionally it can be propelled into the bladder instead of the penis, where it mixes with urine and is eliminated when you pee. This is called retrograde ejaculation. You'll know it's happened to you if nothing comes out when you climax. Men who experience this on a regular basis should see a doctor to find out if it can be corrected, especially if they want to father children. It's also possible that retrograde ejaculation is a symptom of other health problems.

Embryo

Two weeks after conception the fertilized egg attaches itself to the wall of the uterus. At this stage it's called an embryo. For the next 6 weeks the embryo grows rapidly. Limb buds appear, organs begin to develop, and the brain and face start to take shape. By the sixth week the heart is beating steadily. The sex of the child—male or female—is determined between 7 and 12 weeks. At 2 months, the embryo is about 3cm long and is now called a foetus. See Conception, Foetus.

Emergency Contraception ♀
↘ morning-after pill
↘ post-coital ↘ PCP
contraception

If you had sex and didn't use birth control, or you think the birth control you used didn't work, there's a safety net in the form of 2 small pills called emergency contraception. Taken within 24 hours of unprotected intercourse, these pills will reduce your risk of becoming pregnant by 95%. If taken between 48 and 72 hours after unprotected sex, their effectiveness drops to about 58%. They're just like birth control pills, only much stronger. They introduce hormones into your body that prevent an egg from being fertilized. The egg disintegrates and is expelled from your body with your regular vaginal fluids. Your next period should arrive when you'd normally expect it, though it may be a bit early, or more likely, a bit late. If it doesn't arrive, you may be pregnant.

Emergency contraception is exactly what it sounds like; it's for emergencies only. The drugs are extremely strong and shouldn't be used on a regular basis. Emergency contraception doesn't protect against HIV or other sexually transmitted infections.

Q & A ♀

Q: If I don't have emergency contraception, can I take a whole pack of birth control pills instead?

A: No. Ingesting a package of birth control pills all at once will make you very sick.

Q: What happens if you take emergency contraception 4 days after intercourse?

A: The later you take it, the far less effective it is. However, taking emergency contraception on day 4 or 5 won't hurt you and may even reduce the risk of pregnancy, though probably not by much. It's strongly advised not to wait more than 72 hours before taking the first pills.

The ♀ IUD

Another type of emergency contraception is to have a doctor fit you with an IUD within 7 days of unprotected intercourse. But because an IUD can increase your chances of becoming infertile, it's not recommended for use by teenagers.

There's up to a 25% chance emergency protection won't work, which means your best bet if you want to be sure you won't get pregnant is to use birth control correctly.

Emergency Contraception

How to use it

Say you have intercourse with someone, then suddenly realize you might get pregnant. You have exactly 3 days (72 hours) to do something about it. In that time, visit a doctor, who'll give you 2 pills. Take one right away, then 12 hours later take the other one. The earlier the pills are taken, the more effective they'll be. Some regimens consist of 2 pills followed by a further 2, 12 hours later.

Advantages

Inexpensive, easy to use, and very safe. Only 1 in 4 women who use it complain of side effects (see below), which normally disappear an hour or 2 after taking the pills, though they can persist for up to 2 days. Provides a last-minute option.

Disadvantages

Negative side effects include nausea, vomiting, headache, dizziness, and abdominal pain, though these usually disappear shortly after taking the pills. If you vomit within an hour of taking the last pill, you have to take them both again. Serious side effects are very rare and include blood clots, stroke, and heart attack.

Availability

Emergency contraception is available in the United Kingdom at general practice surgeries, family planning clinics, departments of GU medicine and sexual health, and accident and general emergency departments. A version of emergency contraception called 'Levonelle' was made available over the counter from U.K. pharmacies in early 2001. Currently, pharmacists aren't allowed to sell Levonelle-2 to women under 16 years of age. The cost is around £24. Even if the pharmacy doesn't sell the PCP, it may be useful as a first point of contact.

Endometriosis ♀

This is a medical condition that affects the female reproductive system. The uterine lining grows beyond the uterus and attaches to surrounding organs, including the vagina, ovaries, fallopian tubes, bowel, or urinary tract. Symptoms include lower backache, pain during sex, and a long, painful, heavy period. Some women have no symptoms. Endometriosis is often treatable, though not always. In some cases it leads to infertility. Endometriosis doesn't usually show up in women until their 20s.

Q & A ♂

Q: Is there something wrong with me if I get 10 erections a day?

A: There's nothing wrong with you. Some guys get 20 a day and that's normal too. It's also normal to get 3 or 4 a day. Everyone is different.

Erection ♂

↘ hard-on   ↘ stiffy
↘ woody   ↘ boner

By the time you're a teenager you've had hundreds of erections, or maybe it just feels that way. Your penis becomes longer, harder, darker in colour, and stands out from your body. Some penises stand straight out, others curve to the left or right, and some tilt up or down. All of these erections are normal, and no curve, tilt, or angle matters when it comes to intercourse. Very rarely, a penis can be so curved that having sex is difficult. If you think this describes you, see a doctor to make sure there isn't a problem.

You've been getting erections since you were a baby and you'll probably keep on getting them until you're a very old man, or possibly for the rest of your life. They happen when blood fills the spongy cylinders that surround the penis, making it very stiff. An erection can be spontaneous, which means it can pop up in daily situations when sex is the last thing on your mind. If you don't touch your

Erection

Erection

In females

When sexually stimulated, the clitoris becomes engorged with blood in the same way the penis does, resulting in an erection, albeit a much smaller one. At this stage the clitoris is very sensitive, so it pulls back under the hood for protection. The labia also become engorged and swell up. After orgasm, the blood leaves the area and the clitoris and labia quickly resume their normal state.

penis during a spontaneous erection, the hard-on will go away by itself after a short while.

Most erections are the result of stimulation—when your penis is rubbed or stroked in a sexual way. But guys don't always need to be touched to become aroused. Biologically, males have a very sharp visual response, so a sexy image—seen in a photograph or in your imagination or standing right there in front of you—can result in a hard-on. Continuous rubbing will usually bring you to orgasm. Afterwards, your penis will become soft again very quickly. Then you'll have to wait 10 or 15 minutes, or even longer, before you can get an erection again. See Orgasm.

Can't get it up

Penises don't always become erect when you want them to. This leaves many guys feeling desperate, even the first time it happens. But staying soft when you expect rock hard happens to everyone sooner or later. There's usually a simple, short-term cause, such as drinking too much alcohol. This inhibits blood flow to the penis, which means no erection. Drug use can also keep erections down. So can extreme fatigue (too many part-time jobs), stress (there's trouble on the home front), anxiety (you're with the person of your dreams and you're afraid you won't perform), and worry (you didn't get an erection once and you're afraid it will happen again). Occasionally not getting an erection isn't the same as impotence, which is a chronic condition. If you don't worry about it, it probably won't happen again for a long time.

Usually a soft penis that's long won't get much longer when it's erect, while a short soft penis will become considerably longer in its erect state.

Erogenous Zones

For the good of your sexual development, it's important to know your own erogenous zones. These are the areas on your body that are sensitive to sexual stimulation, special places where you love to be caressed, kissed, and tickled. Common erogenous zones for both sexes are the ears, lips, neck, breasts, inner thighs, and genitals. On many guys, the skin between the scrotum and the anus is sexually sensitive, which is also true for the skin between the vaginal opening and the anus on girls. Different people have different erogenous zones, including the backs of the knees or the feet or anywhere else. Do you know what yours are? Actually, the whole human body, from head to toe, is sensitive to touch, making it one big potential erogenous zone.

Erotica

Erotica includes books, magazines, movies, videos, and art that depict sexual activities with sensitivity and artistic appreciation. The purpose of erotica is to stimulate sexual desire and make the experience of having sex more exciting. Pornography is slightly different in that it stimulates or enhances sexual desire using more graphic images. With pornography, there's no artistic intent. But people often don't agree on what art is, which means they often disagree on what is erotica and what is pornography. Anything that turns people on—clothing, food, fantasies, music, fragrance, dance, or even a smile—can be called erotic.

It's not rude to tell your partner where and how you like to be touched. Gently sharing information about what you like will make you closer, physically and emotionally. It will also improve your sex life!

Fallopian Tubes ♀

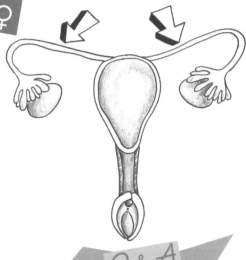

These are two 4-inch-long tubes found in the female pelvis that extend from the uterus like horns from a ram's head. Each tube reaches around to drape its fringe-like end over the ovary that sits just beneath it. When an egg leaves the ovary, it's immediately drawn into the nearest fallopian tube, where it begins a slow journey, travelling at a rate of about 3cm every 24 hours. A sperm has up to 48 hours to find the egg and fertilize it. After fertilization, the egg continues toward the uterus, where it will implant and develop. If the egg gets trapped in the fallopian tube and starts to develop there, you have an ectopic pregnancy, which can be life-threatening. See Ectopic Pregnancy.

Fantasies

It's totally normal and healthy to think about sex and have sexual fantasies. Fantasizing makes you aware of your own desires and teaches you about how your body responds (many people masturbate while they fantasize). It gives you the chance to explore new feelings and to rehearse scenarios you may get to act out one day. It also allows you the freedom to enjoy exciting sexual encounters you'd never attempt in real life. There are no rules, so your imagination can take you wherever you want to go. And you don't have to worry about hurting anyone. Fantasies exist only in your mind; you control the beginning, the middle, and the end, and no one has to know.

Just about everyone has a fantasy life. Some people daydream about romantic

Q & A

Q: Should I tell my boyfriend about my fantasies?

A: Sharing fantasies can be fun, but it's not something everyone enjoys. Before you open up, take a minute to think about how your boyfriend will respond. Will your fantasies make him uncomfortable? Will he feel threatened? It might be a good idea to test the waters by telling him a bit at a time. If he seems cool, tell some more. If he seems bothered in any way, stop. It's okay for fantasies to be private.

Q & A ♀

Q: The only person I ever want to be with is my best friend. I think she feels the same way. Am I a lesbian if sometimes I fantasize about kissing her?

A: You may be a lesbian, but you may not be. To find out, pay attention to your feelings of attraction over a long period of time. If you're consistently attracted to girls and find yourself fantasizing about same-sex activities month after month and year after year, then you may be a lesbian. Or it could be that you just really, really like this girl, but over the long term you discover that you're sexually attracted to guys. Like everyone else, you're on a path of sexual discovery.

encounters with people they already know, or steamy affairs with someone they've never met. Others imagine in graphic detail past sexual experiences. It's not unusual to have same-sex fantasies. This is one of the ways people explore their interest in same-sex activities. This kind of fantasizing doesn't predict anything. It's possible that one day you'll be sexual with someone of your sex, but then again, you may not.

Sometimes people are made uneasy by their fantasies. For example, women who imagine being forced to have sex are scared that this is a sign they want to be raped. It's not. Real rape is nothing at all like the "safe" rape of fantasies, where the person fantasizing is always in control. Some women enjoy these kinds of fantasies because they get to show the full force of their sexual excitement without taking responsibility for it. Guys who dream about being forced to have sex might be fed up with their usual role as the dominant partner. If you have fantasies that are very disturbing to you, it will help to talk about them with someone you trust, like a parent or teacher or counsellor.

Fellatio
↘ **giving head**
↘ **blow job**
↘ **going down**

The Latin verb fellare means "to suck." From there we've derived the word fellatio, which is oral sex that involves kissing, licking, or sucking a penis, or all of the above. Most guys love it, even though some of them can't orgasm that way, no matter how well or how long you do it.

Protection

If you're the one giving the blow job and you're not sure your partner is free of HIV, it's a good idea to use a condom, especially if he plans to come in your mouth. Semen can hold significant amounts of the AIDS virus, which can enter your bloodstream through tiny cuts in your mouth. His penis may also be home to chlamydia, which is another reason to use a condom. Whether you're giving or getting a blow job, gonorrhoea and herpes can easily be transmitted, as can syphilis if

Q & A

Q: If I'm infected with HIV, can I safely give head to my partner?

A: No one knows of any cases where someone has transmitted HIV by performing oral sex. But to be on the safe side, make sure there are no open sores on his penis, or use a condom if it makes you both feel more comfortable.

Q: Is it okay not to use a condom if I take my mouth off his penis before he comes?

A: If you're worried about HIV, the virus can be present in his pre-ejaculate, which is the small amount of fluid that sometimes appears at the tip of the penis before a guy comes. Other infections can also be present in pre-ejaculate. Although the risk of infection is lower with pre-ejaculate than with semen, it's still smart to use a condom. Also, whether or not his penis is in your mouth when he comes, you can still get other sexually transmitted infections, such as herpes, from sucking it.

Q & A

Q: What if I don't want to swallow my boyfriend's semen, but he wants me to?

A: Even if you're in a monogamous relationship and you and your boyfriend both think you're free of sexually transmitted infections, you can never be 100% sure. Ask him to wear a condom. If you end up sucking his naked penis, tell him you don't like swallowing semen, then don't do it. You shouldn't feel pressured into doing anything that makes you feel uncomfortable. If he respects you, he won't make a case out of it.

Q: Can semen get rid of acne?

A: Whether you swallow it or rub it on your skin, semen doesn't have any effect on acne.

Q: Can swallowing semen make you fat?

A: A normal ejaculate amounts to about a tablespoon of semen (maybe a bit less), and contains fewer than 30 calories.

there are open sores present. Hepatitis B can also be transmitted, from saliva to penis or vice versa, though the risk is low. There's also a low risk of catching genital warts.

Covering his penis with a condom is the best protection you can get short of not having sex. Some condoms are made to fit over the testicles too, providing added protection against herpes and genital warts. One way to increase the fun of putting on a condom is to make it part of your sex play. To improve the sensations of the person who's getting the blow job, put a drop or 2 of lubricant into the tip of the condom, but not more or it may slip off. Most lubricants aren't made to be swallowed and they let you know it by tasting terrible, so try buying edible lube, which comes in a variety of flavours. You can also buy flavoured condoms. **See Condoms, Lubricants, Oral Sex.**

STIs you can get: HIV, chlamydia, herpes, gonorrhoea, syphilis, hepatitis B, genital warts

You can cut the risk of contracting HIV from oral sex by keeping your gums, teeth, lips, and throat healthy. If you give unprotected oral sex, avoid flossing or brushing your teeth for a few hours before and afterwards, as these can cause tiny cuts in the mouth, allowing HIV to enter the bloodstream.

Q: Will swallowing semen make my breasts bigger?

A: Nope. There's nothing you can swallow that will make your breasts bigger.

Feminine

This word describes characteristics and behaviours—good and bad—that are traditionally associated with being female. They include selflessness, sensitivity, dependence, mental weakness, compassion, and a willingness to please. Being female is also associated with acting cooperatively and supportively, and being thoughtful, nurturing, emotional, illogical, and sexually passive. Together, these characteristics and behaviours make up a feminine stereotype that's been in effect for hundreds of years. Not surprisingly, large numbers of women identify with this stereotype, which sometimes leads to problems. For example, "feminine" women who are passive in bed and more focused on pleasing than on receiving pleasure are less likely to know themselves sexually and to abandon themselves to the sensations of sex. This can mean an unsatisfying sex life. Fortunately, with each new generation, more and more women are taking responsibility for their own sexual pleasure. This and other changes in the ways women behave are leading to a new definition of feminine.
See Masculine.

See Masculine.

Q & A

Q: I'm a girl, but why don't I feel very feminine?

A: The word "feminine" is a label people use to identify behaviour. It doesn't say anything about who you really are as a woman. As you get to know yourself, you may discover that your femininity has nothing to do with what people think of as feminine. Getting to know yourself is hard, but it's very important if you want to have satisfying relationships and a good sex life. Take some time to focus on yourself. Think about what you like and don't like. Paying too much attention to the way other people label you can be a waste of energy.

Fertility

In males ♂

With your first ejaculation, you're fertile. Even though you're still very young, you have enough sperm in your semen to get someone pregnant.

Q & A

Q: If I've never had my period, can I get pregnant if I have sex? ♀

A: Yes. Many girls ovulate shortly before their very first period starts, which means an egg is available to be fertilized. Since you can't know when your first period will be, it's important that you protect yourself every time you have sex.

Fertility

This is your ability to reproduce.

In females ♀

Your first period is a sign that you may be fertile. Your body is now capable of producing an egg. If fertilized, the egg will develop into a baby. Periods can be irregular (they don't come at the same time every month) for a year or 2 after puberty, which means that each period doesn't always produce an egg. Women are at their most fertile on the day they ovulate and the day after. See Conception, Infertility, Ovulation.

Don't think you won't get pregnant just because your period isn't regular yet. Some irregular periods produce eggs, some don't. Play it safe by always assuming you're fertile.

Fertilization

This is the moment when a sperm penetrates an egg, creating a single cell called a zygote. Inside the zygote is all the genetic material (chromosomes) that go into the making of an individual—half from the father's sperm and half from the mother's egg. The mother's egg is always female. The father's sperm holds the chromosome—male or female—that determines the child's sex. With fertilization, conception has occurred. See Conception, Sex.

For centuries women were blamed, and frequently disposed of, for having daughters and not sons. In fact, the sex of a newly fertilized egg is determined by men's sperm, not women's eggs.

Fetish

For some people, sexual arousal is enhanced by viewing or caressing certain body parts, such as buttocks or feet or breasts. For others, the presence of an object or a piece of clothing, or acting out a make-believe scene, creates extra stimulation. It's common to call these fetishes, but they're not. A true fetish is when someone, usually a man, is unable to feel sexual stimulation or reach orgasm without the presence of the desired clothing (shoes are a classic example), object, or scenario. Having a fetish can seriously get in the way of building a satisfying relationship with another person. If you have a fetish that makes you feel guilty or unhappy, you may find it helpful to see a sex therapist.

Fingering

This is the same as masturbating a woman (make sure your hands are clean). Fingering means sensually touching or exploring her vulva and clitoris. It can also include sliding one or more fingers into the vagina. Because this technique allows direct access to the clitoris, some women find it leads to orgasm faster than sexual intercourse. See G-spot, Hand Job, Masturbation.

Q & A

Q: How does someone get rid of a fetish?

A: It's very hard to get rid of a sexual fetish. In most cases, fetishes take root at a young age and are a means of dealing with anxiety. When this is the case, the anxiety needs to be identified and new ways need to be found to become sexually aroused. This is difficult to do, partly because it's hard to deny the pleasure the fetish brings while exploring new possibilities. Depending on the type of fetish and how long it's been around, seeing a sex therapist may help.

Fingering
Protection

If you're unsure of your partner's STI status, after fingering her, wash your hands well before touching your own genitals, eyes, nose, or mouth. If you don't have any open cuts or sores on your hands, you can't get HIV from fingering, and you can't give it if you're infected.

A: By the time they have intercourse, many girls will have stretched or lost their hymen through sports or as a result of putting in tampons. Some girls don't have a hymen to begin with. If your hymen is still intact, it could hurt a bit as the penis stretches or tears it. First sex, or sex at any time, can also be painful if you're not sufficiently aroused (your vagina isn't relaxed and lubricated). This problem can be dealt with by sensitive, prolonged foreplay. See Hymen.

First Sex

Your first time having sex is a big deal and it would be really great if it went well. Good first sex has a better chance of leading to a good sex life than bad first sex, which can leave you feeling guilty, angry, or hurt. Bad first sex can give a person negative feelings about sex in general. No one wants that. But don't expect fireworks from first sex. Not that fireworks aren't possible, they're just not probable. Good first sex is exactly that: good. Later, practice makes perfect. Of course, if your first time is not-so-good, it's possible to get over it and get onto the right track. Making a mistake is just another way of finding out what you really want.

To improve the odds of having good first sex you need to know: who you want to sleep with, why you want to sleep with that person, when and where you want to do it, and what kind of protection you and your partner will use. For all of the above, you need your partner's agreement, which means that you and your partner need to communicate. It will also help if you're both comfortable with your feelings of desire and have some knowledge of your own and each other's bodies. Will you be able to show your partner what makes you feel good? Have you read up on what will make him or her feel good? Knowing the answers to these questions will help you to be more relaxed, and relaxation goes a long way to creating a good first experience. See Ready for Sex.

For females

It's common for girls who are virgins to feel a lot of pressure from their peers to have intercourse. When they finally give in, these girls often leave the decision about whether or not to use protection up to the guy. Because he's the one who initiated the sex, he controls the experience. When a guy says

First Sex

he doesn't want to use protection, it's typical for the girl not to insist on it. Maybe she's afraid of losing him, or she doesn't want to look stupid. Or maybe she doesn't want to bother with protection either. As a result, she leaves herself open to pregnancy and infections. Girls who make up their own minds about when they want to have sex, whether it's the first time or the tenth, are far more likely to protect themselves.

For males ♂

Despite all the physical changes that happen to guys in puberty, there's not one development that signals sexual maturity (in girls, sexual maturity is signalled by menstruation). For many guys, having intercourse is the first real sign of being a man, and the pressure to "perform" can be significant. It's an important moment. At this point, many guys aren't as interested in the relationship or in protection as they are in the sex. While this is normal, it's good to remember that "relationship" and protection may be foremost in the mind of your partner.

Some guys worry they won't be good at sex or won't be able to get an erection in the first place. Others feel intimidated by the maturity they see in female bodies. The trick is not to worry too much about these things. First sex may not be perfect, but everything will happen more or less as it's supposed to, especially if you pay attention to what's going on with your partner. You should also be sensitive to the role you play with regard to protection. If you're with someone who seems hesitant to bring up the topic, make it clear that you support using it. If you're both protected, you'll probably feel more relaxed, which always improves sex.

The first time is scary for guys too. Just like a girl who's having sex for the first time, a guy who's never done it before is completely in the dark. He might pretend to be in control when he really doesn't feel that way at all.

Fisting

Putting your hand or fist into someone's vagina or rectum is called fisting. This kind of penetration offers pleasure to some people, but pain to many others. Fisting is almost always harmful to the vagina and rectum, which are lined with soft, fragile tissue that tears easily. It can also lead to a ruptured anal sphincter and a perforated colon. The cervix can also be damaged.

Foreplay Q&A

Q: How can I find out what to do to make foreplay more interesting and exciting?

A: There are many excellent sex books in libraries and bookshops that can tell you everything you need to know. The more information you have about how your body works, and how your partner's body works, the more confident you'll be about trying new things. Another benefit of arming yourself with information is that it may help you feel less shy about asking your partner what she or he likes.

Foetus

At the beginning of the third month of pregnancy the developing embryo is called a foetus. This is the baby's medical name until birth. See Embryo.

Foreplay

This word describes all the sexually pleasing things people do with each other before having intercourse, if they decide to go that far. One of the keys to good foreplay is having plenty of time. Another is being relaxed. Relaxation won't be a problem if you know your body and you're comfortable with exploring your sexuality. It also helps if you trust and really like your partner and the feelings are mutual. If you're planning to have sex, foreplay has to include an awareness of who's going to put on what protection at what moment. For some people, foreplay is the best part of sex.

Foreplay plays an essential role in preparing the body for intercourse—guys get an erection (if they don't already have one) and girls become lubricated, which can take a lot longer than it takes a penis to jump to attention. But it's possible for 2 people to be so instantly excited that foreplay isn't needed to enhance arousal. If that's the case, it's still a wonderful way to be intimate with your partner. Activities include hand-holding, kissing (there are so many different ways to kiss and places to kiss, this activity alone can take up a lot of time), touching, caressing, massaging, hugging, body pressing, and mutual masturbation. You don't need to be naked to enjoy great foreplay.

Foreskin ♂

This is the loose skin that covers the end of your penis, either totally or partially. All boys are born with a foreskin, but some have it removed shortly after birth for religious or cultural reasons in a procedure called circumcision. Sometimes circumcision is performed later in childhood, or even in adulthood, for medical reasons. When a penis that isn't circumcised becomes erect, the foreskin is pulled back to expose the head.

Washing under the foreskin regularly is important because smegma can collect there, causing a bad smell or an infection. Washing is also necessary before presenting your penis for oral sex. When putting on a condom, always pull back your foreskin first. See Circumcision, Smegma.

French Kissing

↘snogging
↘deep kissing
↘wet kissing

This is when 2 people kiss with their mouths open and their tongues touching. French kissing can be a gentle prodding of the other person's tongue or a passionate and prolonged exploration of their lips and the inside of their mouth. The deeper the French kiss, the more saliva gets exchanged, but unless things get really wet and sloppy, you don't notice it. If the French kissing is good, where the saliva is going is the last thing on your mind.

STIs you can get:
hepatitis B,
herpes (cold sores),
possibly mononucleosis

Q & A

Q: Can I give my boyfriend pleasure by playing with his foreskin?

A: The foreskin doesn't feel much. What's really sensitive is the glans, which is just underneath the foreskin. If you want to touch the glans, make sure to pull back the foreskin slowly. Depending on how aroused your boyfriend is, there may not be enough lubrication between the glans and the foreskin to allow it to come back easily. If it's dry, it will probably hurt.

Q: Can the foreskin be too tight?

A: In rare cases it can, sometimes as a result of certain skin conditions. A foreskin that's too tight can stop you from having an erection. See a doctor to find a solution to this problem.

Q: Does a guy's frenulum break the first time he has sex?

A: The frenulum almost always stays intact, though very rarely it can tear or bleed during poorly lubricated sex. This has nothing to do with having sex for the first time.

Q: Can a person get HIV from french kissing?

A: The saliva of someone infected with HIV has a very small amount of the AIDS virus, probably too small to infect another person. The risk increases when there's blood-to-blood contact through cuts in the mouth.

Frenulum ♂

At the top of your penis, just on the underside, there's a small strip of skin that connects the foreskin to the head. This is the frenulum. In a circumcised penis, it connects the head of the penis to the shaft. There's a high concentration of nerve endings in the frenulum, which means it's extremely sensitive. Some guys actually find it too sensitive and prefer to be stimulated on other parts of the penis.

Frigidity

Not so long ago women who abstained from sex or who couldn't have orgasms, or who weren't as interested in sex as their partners, were labelled frigid. Frigidity was considered to be a nasty condition that only women suffered from. Frequently, these women were looked down upon. Over time, the notion that frigidity was a condition was proven false. For one thing, not everyone has the same sex drive, and a low sex drive is as normal as a high one. Also, people now understand that almost all women are able to have orgasms, it's just that some don't know how. This should come as no surprise. For centuries the majority of women were discouraged from exploring their bodies and feeling sexual pleasure. Women's role was to give pleasure, not receive it. Even today, many women are uncomfortable telling their partners what feels good. Learning to masturbate and becoming adept at self-pleasuring is an excellent way to get better at climaxing with a partner. On the other hand, if you don't climax but the sex is still good and you're satisfied, there's no problem.

Unfortunately, the concept of frigidity hasn't entirely disappeared. Once in a while, people who aren't getting the sex they want use the term "frigid" to describe the women, or sometimes men, who refuse to have sex with them. Today, remarks about frigidity are considered to be ignorant.
See Arousal, Desire, Masturbation.

Q: Do guys have a G-spot?

A: Some people call the prostate gland the male G-spot. You can stimulate it by stroking your partner's skin between his scrotum and anus, or you can stroke it from the inside, through the wall of the rectum, by pushing gently toward the scrotum. The prostate is about the size and shape of a walnut.

G-spot

Inside a woman's vagina there's a spot that's particularly sensitive to sexual stimulation. To find it, reach a finger 1 1/2 to 3 inches inside the vagina and push toward her belly button. If she feels like peeing, you've discovered her G-spot, says Dr Ernst Grafenberg, who first wrote about it in the 1940s. Rubbing this area from inside the vagina can increase sexual excitement and contribute to orgasm. Some people don't believe the G-spot exists, claiming that female genitals have many sensitive areas. Others simply use the term to describe the place in their body that makes them feel sexiest.

Gay

The word "gay" has had sexual connotations for hundreds of years, but it wasn't until the 1960s that it was popularly used to describe men and women whose feelings of sexual desire were directed at people of the same sex. In the 1970s, however, lesbians protested that gay events and organizations either ignored women's concerns or excluded women's participation outright. From that time on, lesbians went their own way, and "gay" came to refer primarily to men who loved men and who identified with the new gay culture and the burgeoning gay rights movement. Today, gay culture is politically organized and many gay men are very active in caring for the well-being of their community. To find out where to go to learn more about this community, see Resources at the end of the book. See Homosexual, Lesbian, Queer.

Gender

There are 2 sexes: male and female. The words "male" and "female" are also used to describe the 2 different genders. Despite this similarity, sex and gender aren't the same thing. Sex is about identifying the anatomy. Gender is about identifying the person.

Understanding others

The first thing we do when we meet someone new is identify that person's sex as male or female. The next thing we do, without even realizing it, is make assumptions about the kinds of behaviours and attitudes that person will have based on stereotypes we've learned about his or her sex. If he's male, we might expect him to be aggressive, confident, and independent. If she's female, we might expect her to be thoughtful, sympathetic, and caring. Our expectations are something we learned at a very early age: boys act one way, girls act another.

There are words to describe the typical ways boys and girls act. The word for boys is "masculine." For girls, it's "feminine." Throughout history, males who've acted feminine and females who've acted masculine have often been ridiculed or rejected. This still happens today, though it's less common. These days men and women are more likely to choose behaviours that suit their personality, regardless of whether these behaviours are traditionally masculine or feminine. For example, more men are comfortable showing compassion, while more women allow themselves to be openly competitive. Because of this mixing of behaviours, it's harder to know what to expect when you meet someone new. **See Androgyny, Feminine, Masculine, Sex.**

Understanding yourself

The way people identify themselves usually matches up with their body parts (I'm female, I have breasts and a vagina; I'm male, I have a penis). This is because biology plays a large part in determining how people feel. But sometimes biology goes astray and individuals develop with the feelings of one sex and the genitalia of another (I'm female, I have a penis; I'm male, I have a vagina). This can be very confusing, not only for the individual, but also for friends and relatives who are able to identify the sex, but aren't sure what kind of behaviour to expect.

Most people believe that gender isn't simply a matter of biology, and that the way parents raise their children also plays a role. Parents have preconceived ideas about how girls and boys are different, and day after day they communicate their ideas to their children. For example, it's common for parents to take great delight in their daughter's hair and pretty clothing (emphasizing her appearance), while complimenting their son on his athletic abilities (emphasizing his strength).

The majority of children identify strongly with one gender or the other by the age of 4. Is this because their gender was biologically determined or because they "learned" their gender through social interactions? Most researchers believe that both factors play a part. Some people believe that gender is entirely environmental and artificial. **See Hermaphrodite, Queer, Transgendered, Transsexual.**

Gender Roles

You're probably familiar with the roles played by most women throughout history, such as mother, caregiver, servant, ornament, and sexual dependent. The roles played by most men included father, provider, protector, scholar, artist, inventor, explorer, warrior, and many more. These are called gender roles, or sex roles. In recent times, as women have joined the work force in large numbers and some men have stayed home to look after children, gender roles have become less rigid, though they haven't disappeared. For many gays and lesbians, gender roles are oppressive because they represent society's unrealistic expectations. Some gays and lesbians go so far as to denounce them as bogus and irrelevant, though it's not uncommon for others to comfortably identify with one or the other of the roles.

> Keeping an open mind means not judging people according to their sex when you first meet them. Instead, you let them show you who they are by their words and actions.

Genital Warts
↘venereal warts

In terms of warts, you probably thought all you had to worry about were those ugly little bumps that sometimes show up on people's hands or feet. Known as common warts, they're caused by several related viruses that are spread through casual contact. A different group of viruses cause another kind of wart to grow on people's skin. It's called a genital wart and is spread through sexual contact. Genital warts look a lot like common warts. People who are infected with genital warts often develop clusters of warts on their genitals, around their anus, and very occasionally around their mouth. Both groups of viruses fall under the heading human papillomavirus (HPV), which is a family of viruses that contains over 100 different types.

Genital warts are very, very contagious. To become infected, all you have to do is touch your skin to someone's warts. That's easy to avoid, you think. When you see the warts, you won't touch them, right? The problem is, sometimes they only grow inside the vagina or anus, where they aren't visible. To make matters worse, genital warts on your skin can be so tiny that you can't see them, even if you're looking. Anyway, lots of people don't look, especially when they have sex in the dark. That's why genital warts is one of the fastest-growing sexually transmitted infections in the United Kingdom.

Besides being unsightly, genital warts can be painful if rubbed (especially if they're inside the vagina), and sometimes they itch. In addition to causing genital warts, certain types of HPV can cause cervical pre-cancer and cancer. If you have genital warts, this does not automatically mean that you're at an increased risk of developing cervical cancer. In the United Kingdom, patients with genital warts are advised to have cervical smears only every 3 to 4 years (that is, no more frequently than patients without genital warts).

You can catch genital warts, and other strains of HPV, from any kind of skin contact. This includes intercourse, anal sex, and mutual masturbation. If you perform oral sex on someone who has them, you could develop them on your mouth. If that happens, anyone you kiss or perform oral sex on is at risk of getting them too. If you catch genital warts, you won't know you're infected right away. It usually takes 3 months for the warts to develop, though they sometimes show up 3 weeks later, and in other cases, a year or more later. When the warts first appear, it's also possible to self-infect a different part of your genitals by touching infected skin, then touching uninfected skin. Usually, over time, the body develops antibodies to the virus and self-infection becomes unlikely.

Q & A ♂

Q: Are the white spots on my penis genital warts?

A: The small, shiny white spots on the head of your penis are normal and harmless. They're called pearly papules and are nothing to worry about.

Q: Will genital warts ♀ make me infertile?

A: You can still get pregnant if you have genital warts, even if the warts are growing inside your vagina. Because it's possible to transmit the virus to your baby during birth, make sure your doctor knows about the infection.

Smokers who are infected with HPV usually develop more warts than non-smokers do. This is because smoking suppresses the immune system, making it easier for the virus to spread.

In females ♀

Look for genital warts to appear on your vaginal lips (vulva) or on the skin between your vaginal opening and anus (the perineum). They can also pop up inside your vagina or anus and on your cervix. In fact, genital warts can develop anywhere on your skin that has come into contact with the warts of an infected partner. Sometimes a cervical smear will show abnormal cell growth on your cervix caused by HPV, and that's how you'll find out you have it. Women with genital warts do not require more frequent cervical smears. If evidence of HPV is found on a cervical smear, a re-check is usually advised 6 months later. Women are more susceptible than men to catching HPV.

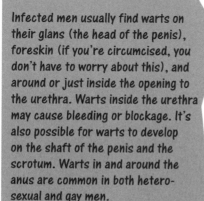

In males ♂

Infected men usually find warts on their glans (the head of the penis), foreskin (if you're circumcised, you don't have to worry about this), and around or just inside the opening to the urethra. Warts inside the urethra may cause bleeding or blockage. It's also possible for warts to develop on the shaft of the penis and the scrotum. Warts in and around the anus are common in both hetero-sexual and gay men.

Getting tested

If you see a wart or cluster of warts in your genital area, visit a doctor, who should be able to make a visual diagnosis. If you've got the microscopic kind, he or she may examine your skin with a special instrument or put a solution on the area where warts are suspected. The solution may turn the warts white. Women often find out they have the genital warts virus (HPV) after a cervical smear, when their test results show an abnormality. Testing for HPV is currently not routinely undertaken in the United Kingdom.

Treatment

There's no cure for genital warts. It's possible the warts will go away on their own, but even if they do, the virus will probably remain in your body. Current treatment focuses on removing the warts. If they're not present, there's less chance the virus will be transmitted. Also, removal lowers the likelihood of complications due to an overgrowth of warts. You and your doctor will decide what's the best way to remove them—by freezing or burning them off, treating them with chemicals, or cutting them out in surgery. Because recurrence is common, watch for new warts to appear over the next months, then have those removed too.

Prevention

You can avoid genital warts by never touching another person's warts. Because so many millions of people have them and because the warts are often invisible or spread over large skin areas, this means not having sex unless you're sure your partner is free of the infection. A condom or dam may protect you, though only if your partner's warts are on areas of the skin that are covered. Another way to lower your risk is to keep your immune system strong through rest, exercise, and good nutrition. Even if you already have HPV, a strong immune system will slow the spread of warts.

Genitals

The sex organs you find between your legs. Also called genitalia.

In females

A girl's genitals are found in the area of her vulva. They include her labia majora and minora, the opening to her vagina, the opening to her urethra, and her clitoris.

In males

A boy's genitals include his penis and scrotum.

Gonads

↘sex glands
↘reproductive
    organs

After fertilization, several weeks pass before the biological sex of an embryo reveals itself. This usually happens in the sixth week of pregnancy, with the development of either female or male gonads. The female gonads are the ovaries, which produce eggs and female sex hormones. The male gonads are the testes, which produce sperm and male sex hormones. The production of female hormones influences the development of female genitalia, while the production of male hormones influences the development of male genitalia.

♀ Females

A doctor or nurse will examine you to see if your cervix is inflamed. You'll have secretions taken from your mouth, ure-thra, cervix, or anus with a swab (a quick swipe usually does it). The secretions will be tested for gonococcus. It's also possible to have a urine test, though this kind of testing isn't widely available. You should be able to have the results of your test within the week.

♂ Males

A thin swab is very briefly inserted into the opening at the tip of your penis. The swab picks up secretions, which will later be tested in the laboratory for gonococcus. In departments of GU medicine and sexual health, gonorrhoea may be diagnosed while you wait by examining secretions under the microscope.

Anyone who thinks they may have been in contact with gonorrhoea should seek advice from a department of GU medicine or sexual health.

Gonorrhoea
↘the drip ↘the clap ↘a dose

This is a very common, curable infection that's transmit-ted from one person to another through unprotected oral sex, anal sex, and intercourse. It's caused by bean-shaped bacteria that invade the moist, warm membranes of the genitals, anus, and throat. The bacteria—known as gonococcus—thrive in this environment. Away from it, they die almost immediately.

Many people with gonorrhoea don't have symp-toms in the early stages, but for those who do, the symptoms show up 2 to 10 days after infection. Without symptoms, people don't realize they have gonorrhoea, so it doesn't get treated. Left alone, gonorrhoea may move from being an infection to being a serious disease. The result can be complications that include many unpleasant symptoms and even sterility. Untreated, gonorrhoea is also easily spread from partner to partner.

If you aren't infected the first time you sleep with someone who has gonorrhoea, you have a greater chance of being infected the second time, and your risk continues to rise with each time you have sex. It's also possible to spread the infection to your eyes by touching the discharge from a penis, then touching your finger to your eye.

Infection as a result of intercourse
In females ♀

Of infected women, 80% don't have any symptoms in the early stages, even though their cervix is inflamed. They only realize something is wrong when they notice the discomforts of pelvic inflammatory disease (PID), a serious condition that develops when gonorrhoea isn't treated. A significant number of girls and women with PID become infertile or suffer an ectopic pregnancy, which can be deadly. Women with symptoms may notice a yellow or yellow-green discharge on their underwear, or their vulva may be irritated.

Gonorrhoea

In males

Some guys don't have symptoms, but about 80% do. The symptoms include a bad-smelling, cloudy discharge that drips from the opening at the tip of your penis, a burning feeling when you pee, and the need to pee often. If the bacteria aren't stopped, within 4 weeks they might make themselves comfortable deeper inside your body. At this point you may feel swelling and tenderness in your groin. Complications can include scarring that will leave you unable to father a child.

Infection as a result of oral sex
In males and females

The only symptom is a sore throat that shows up several days after infection, though most people who are infected never develop this symptom.

Infection as a result of anal sex
In males and females

In most cases symptoms aren't present, and even when they exist, they're often not noticed because of their location. Symptoms include an anal discharge, bowel disorders, tenderness just inside the rectum, and itching.

Treatment

Gonorrhoea is cured with one large dose of antibiotics, but there's a problem—the bacteria are becoming resistant to more and more of the antibiotics used in treatment. Researchers are working around the clock to make sure a new antibiotic is in the wings should the other ones fail.

Common wisdom says that if your partner is being treated, you should get treated too. You'll both probably be treated for chlamydia at the same time as it's often present alongside gonorrhoea. A follow-up test is recommended 3 to 7 days later to make sure the antibiotic worked. Despite successful treatment, you can get infected again at any time.

About 20,000 new cases of gonorrhoea are reported every year in the United Kingdom, and most of these involve people between the ages of 15 and 24.

If you have gonorrhoea, there's a good chance you have chlamydia, and vice versa.

You can't catch gonorrhoea from a toilet seat.

Prevention

People being treated for gonorrhoea should avoid vaginal, anal, and oral sex. Only when a follow-up test has proven negative should they resume their normal sex lives. If you test positive for gonorrhoea, tell your previous partners about the infection so that they can go for treatment too. Using a condom or diaphragm drastically reduces the chances of infection.

Gynaecologist

If you have a consultation with a gynaecologist, they will take your sexual history, and may ask rather personal details about your periods and the kind of contraception you use. There is normally a pelvic examination to check up on the heatlh of your genital organs. If the gynae-cologist is male, you can request a female nurse to be present if that makes you feel more comfortable. Don't be afraid to ask as many questions as you need to during the examination.

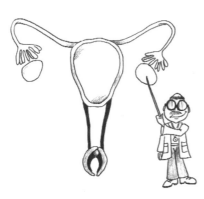

GUM Clinic

↘genitourinary
    medicine clinic
↘STD clinic
↘special clinic
↘VD clinic
↘sexual health clinic

This is where to go if you think you have an STI, are concerned about your sexual health, or would like a check-up.

Many GUM clinics see people without appointments, but it's best to ring first and check. When you arrive, you'll be asked to register. But don't worry, you can give as much or as little information as you like—all health services are completely confidential and no information will be passed on without your permission.

The doctor will ask you questions about your "sexual history" to help decide which tests need to be done. It's important to answer the questions truthfully, even if you feel embarrassed—the doctor won't judge you but is there to help.

All advice, information and treatment is free. For details of your nearest GUM clinic, look in the telephone directory or try www.shastd.org.uk. See STIs.

Gynaecologist ♀

This is a doctor who specializes in female reproductive health. While many G.P.s are highly capable in this area, you may be referred to a gynaecologist by your G.P. for more specialized care and examination. See Doctors.

Hand Job

Giving a guy a hand job is the same as masturbating him. It means using your hand to stroke or rub his penis, usually until he ejaculates. It's normal for teenage guys to be so excited that they ejaculate at the first touch of your hand or a few seconds later. See Fingering, Masturbation.

Protection

Because there's always bacteria around the genitals, it's a good idea to wash your hands after giving someone a hand job. It's even more important if there's a possibility your partner has herpes or genital warts. If he does and you touch him, then touch your own genitals, eyes, nose, or mouth, you could catch the infection.

If you don't have any open cuts or sores on your hands, you can't get HIV from giving someone a hand job, and you can't give it if you're infected. If you do have cuts, you can reduce the risk of contracting HIV by asking your partner to wear a condom.

Hepatitis

There are 3 main types of hepatitis: A, B, and C. Each of these types is caused by a virus that enters the body and attacks the liver. The 3 hepatitis viruses are transmitted differently and each affects the body in its own way.

Hepatitis A

People who are infected with hepatitis A carry the virus in their faeces. The virus is spread when the germs from contaminated faeces are ingested by a second person. This can happen in several ways, including when someone who's infected doesn't wash his or her hands after going to the bathroom, and then prepares food for others. Sexually, there are 4 ways that people can end up with germs from their partner's faeces in their mouth: through oral sex, oral-anal sex (rimming), anal sex (after sex, the partner touches his hand to his penis, then puts his hand to his mouth), and anal-finger sex (after sex, the partner touches his finger to his mouth).

Some people never know they're infected because they don't have symptoms. Others get flu-like symptoms 2 to 6 weeks after infection and think they have the flu. But they know something is up when their faeces turn pale and their urine darkens in colour. This happens as a result of the liver being infected. As the infection progresses, many hepatitis victims become jaundiced, which means their skin and the whites of their eyes turn yellowish. Becoming jaundiced usually means that recovery is just around the corner. Hepatitis A rarely leads to serious complications.

Getting tested

There's no test for hepatitis A. By the time people feel sick enough to see a doctor, they're already getting better.

Hepatitis A

To get over hepatitis A, you need to rest, avoid stress, and eat plenty of good foods. The illness goes away by itself in several weeks, though for some people it can be months before they feel completely well again. One good thing about hepatitis A is that getting it once creates an immunity in the body, which means a person can't get it again. But it's still possible to contract hepatitis B or C.

Prevention

A safe, effective vaccine to prevent hepatitis A has been available for several years. If you aren't vaccinated, wear a condom during anal sex and use a dam or latex glove for other anus-related activities. Make sure you wash your hands well with soap and water if there's a chance they've come into contact with faeces. If you haven't been vaccinated, don't have sex with anyone who looks jaundiced.

Treatment

The treatment for hepatitis B is to rest, avoid stress, and eat healthy foods. It's also necessary to avoid drugs and alcohol, which can damage the liver. Recovery usually takes between 3 and 4 months. Very severe cases can lead to hospitalization and even death. Fortunately, once people get hepatitis B, they're immune for life. But it's still possible to contract hepatitis A and C.

Prevention

A safe vaccine is available that prevents the transmission of the infection in 95% of cases. There are 3 injections over 6 months, all of them in the shoulder. In the U.K., the vaccine is recommended only for those at particular risk of coming into contact with the infection. If you haven't been vaccinated, don't kiss or have sex with anyone who looks jaundiced, and when you do have sex, use a condom. Also, don't use things that could have someone else's blood on it, such as toothbrushes, razors, drug-injection needles, and needles used in body piercing and tattooing. If you're getting a tattoo or body piercing, make sure you go to a place where clean needles are guaranteed.

Hepatitis B

People who are infected with hepatitis B carry the virus in their blood and body fluids. Highly contagious, the virus is easily spread when the infected fluids—semen, blood, vaginal fluids, or saliva—enter a second person's body through cuts, sores, or any other opening such as the mouth, vagina, or anus. Sexually, this can happen during kissing, intercourse, anal sex, and oral sex. Non-sexually, it frequently happens when people share needles to inject drugs. Hepatitis B usually heals on its own, though serious complications can occur before the healing begins. These include liver failure, which you can die from, and cancer of the liver.

Some people with hepatitis B never have symptoms. In others, symptoms show up 6 weeks to 6 months after infection. They include fatigue, sore throat, headaches, diarrhoea, poor appetite, achy muscles, and an upset stomach. In some cases the symptoms are more severe and include high fever, vomiting, and abdominal pains. It's possible to be so tired that you can't get out of bed. Because the liver is infected, faeces become pale and urine darkens in colour. Finally, many hepatitis victims become jaundiced, which is when their skin and the whites of their eyes turn slightly yellow.

Getting tested

The presence of hepatitis B is determined through a blood test. More blood tests may be needed to find out if there's been liver damage. After recovery, the doctor may request 1 or 2 additional blood tests to find out if the person who had the disease has become a carrier. This happens in rare cases, and though carriers have no symptoms, they can still transmit the virus.

Hepatitis C

People who are infected with hepatitis C carry the virus in their blood. Recent studies suggest that it's also carried in semen and possibly vaginal fluids, but this hasn't been proved. The virus is usually spread when infected blood enters the bloodstream of a second person through sharing drug paraphernalia such as needles, spoons, and straws. Hepatitis C is rarely transmitted sexually, though it can pass from one person to another during intercourse if the infected partner is a menstruating woman and her menstrual fluid touches cuts or tears on her partner's skin. It's possible there are other ways the virus is spread through sexual contact, but they aren't well understood. Anal sex and fisting are considered to be higher risk activities because they can cause tears in the rectum. Most people who become infected with hepatitis C have the virus for the rest of their lives.

Symptoms of hepatitis C usually develop 10 or 15 years after infection, though some people go their entire lives without any signs that they have it. The symptoms, which can come and go, include fatigue, nausea, loss of appetite, vomiting, abdominal pain, aching muscles, fever, diarrhoea, and jaundice. The worst symptom is serious liver damage, which occurs in up to 25% of people with the disease.

Getting tested

Hepatitis C is detected through blood tests. People who've shared drug paraphernalia or have had a tattoo or body piercing at a shop that didn't guarantee clean needles should ask their doctor to give them one or more of these tests (one test isn't always conclusive). Testing is also a good idea if you've had sex with someone already infected with the disease, or if you've used their razor or toothbrush.

Treatment

Drug treatments for chronic hepatitis C are available, but they don't work in everyone and they almost always have side effects. Because alcohol is hard on the liver, people with hepatitis C should avoid drinking beer, wine, and spirits.

Prevention

There's no vaccine against hepatitis C. The best prevention is to avoid using toothbrushes, razors, drug paraphernalia, or anything else that might have someone else's blood on it. And when getting a body piercing or tattoo, make sure the needles are clean. You can also protect yourself by practising safer sex, in other words, by limiting your number of partners and using condoms.

Hepatitis C cannot be transmitted through kissing, hugging, shaking hands, coughing, sneezing, sharing utensils or towels, or any other kind of casual contact.

Hermaphrodite

This term is used to describe people who are born with a combination of male and female genitalia, or with genitalia that are only partially formed. Later, during adolescence, hermaphrodites may or may not develop female-type breasts. As adults, some will be sterile, while others will be able to conceive and have children. Depending on the form this condition takes, some individuals feel male, others feel female. The term hermaphrodite comes from the Greek god Hermaphroditus, whose union with a nymph left him with both male and female characteristics.

The origins of hermaphroditism can be traced back to the days and weeks following conception, when the embryo is undergoing major growth. At this stage, either the sex chromosomes combine in unusual ways or hormonal abnormalities affect the development of the embryo. Recently, medical technology has come up with options that can make life easier for people with this condition, such as removing or reconstructing genitalia, though not everyone feels the need to have this kind of surgery. See Gender, Sex.

Herpes

Millions of people have herpes, which is caused by a virus that's easily passed from one person to another when they touch. The herpes simplex-1 virus causes cold sores, though most people don't think of herpes when they see someone with sores around their mouth. When they think of herpes, it's always the genital kind that worries them, the kind that causes blisters and sores to appear on their penis, vagina, or anus. This is the herpes simplex-2 virus. It's also possible to pass the herpes simplex-1 virus to your partner's genitals if you're infected and you give your partner oral sex. Other ways to contract herpes are through kissing, intercourse, anal sex, and mutual masturbation.

To get herpes, you have to touch skin that's infected. This would be easier to avoid if infected skin always looked different from healthy skin. Mostly it does—when the sores are present, they're very visible. But skin can also be infected when there are no sores present. This is called viral shedding. It means that healthy-looking skin can be infected with the virus, and if you touch it, you'll probably catch it. The virus is also present in semen and vaginal fluids.

The main symptom of herpes is an outbreak of sores on your skin. It's often preceded by a burning or itching sensation. People who get headachy and feverish around this time think they're coming down with the flu. The sores (in small clusters) last for 2 to 3 weeks, during which time they crack and ooze liquid and maybe bleed. They can be painful. You can also have trouble urinating. But you can't count on these symptoms to let you know you have herpes. Sometimes sores never show up. Sometimes they only arrive months after infection. Whether you have them or not, it's still possible to be contagious.

Usually the first outbreak is the nastiest. Some people never have another one. In other people, outbreaks can occur at different periods in their lives, though they're rarely as painful as the first one.

In females

Most women who catch herpes are infected during intercourse and develop sores on their vaginal lips (vulva). Sores can also develop inside the vagina, in the belly button, in and around the anus, and on the clitoris, cervix, buttocks, and thighs. Sores may be accompanied by an increase in vaginal discharge. Pregnant women have to be watchful because an outbreak of sores can lead to miscarriage or a delivery that's dangerously early. If you're pregnant and have herpes, it's very important to tell your doctor.

In males

Sores typically show up on the head and shaft of the penis, though they can also develop in and around the anus and on the scrotum, buttocks, and thighs.

Prevention

Researchers are working on a vaccine. In the meantime, the best protection is to use a condom or to avoid sexual contact altogether if your partner has sores on his or her mouth or genitals. Condoms offer good protection if the sores are limited to the penis, vagina, or anus; unfortunately, they offer none against sores that are present on other skin areas. When the sores are gone, there's much less risk of catching the infection. A less obvious but very important form of protection is to stay rested and healthy. This will keep your immune system strong and you'll be less likely to catch infections, even if you're exposed.

Q & A

Q: Can I get pregnant if I have herpes?

A: Genital herpes won't stop you from getting pregnant. Nor will it stop guys who have it from getting a girl pregnant.

Getting tested

The best time to see a doctor is as soon as the sores appear. The doctor may be able to immediately identify the infection, but sometimes a test is needed. This involves taking a swab from the sores, which can be uncomfortable. The swab then goes to a lab to be examined. You should find out the cause of your sores in a week or 2. There are now blood tests available to determine whether you have been infected with herpes, but they can't always tell you whether your genital symptoms are due to herpes.

Treatment

There's no cure for herpes, at least not yet. Once the virus is in your body, you can't get rid of it. You can even spread the virus from one part of your body to another by touching an infected area, then touching another part of your body (herpes virus in the eye can lead to blindness). To avoid re-infecting yourself, keep your hands washed and clean, especially during the first outbreak. By the time a second outbreak occurs, your body may have developed antibodies that will protect other areas from infection.

Treatments for herpes focus on 2 things: getting you through outbreaks as painlessly as possible, and keeping outbreaks to a minimum. To do the former, keep the sores clean and dry. Also, your doctor may be able to recommend a soothing cream or ointment that can be applied to the sores. Very occasionally, people with herpes experience frequent occurences – in which case, medication can be taken to prevent outbreaks. You need to discuss this with your doctor or a specialist in a GU medicine or sexual health clinic. Keeping your stress level down and getting as much sleep as possible is also helpful, as is staying out of the sun. Too much sun can activate the virus, causing sores to erupt.

Heterosexual

↘hetero

↘straight

This word describes someone who feels romantically and sexually attracted to people of the opposite sex. Girls feel curious about guys and want to be with them, emotionally and sexually, and guys feel curious about girls and want to be with them, sexually and emotionally. People who are heterosexual can sometimes have same-sex thoughts and feelings and occasionally act on them, but their strongest desire is for people of the other sex.

Being heterosexual doesn't mean you can't get infected with HIV and other sexually transmitted infections. Infections can happen to anyone, regardless of sexual orientation. See Bisexual, Gay, Homosexual, Lesbian, Queer.

Q: Is there a vaccine for HIV?

A: As yet there is no HIV vaccine on the market, though one is being tested on humans (for safety, not for effectiveness). Researchers say it will be many years before an HIV vaccine is ready for use.

Q: If I'm HIV-positive, is it okay to have unprotected sex with someone who's also HIV-positive?

A: It's not okay. You still have to practise safer sex. Sleeping with someone who's infected with HIV can give you even more of the virus, and your body is having enough trouble fighting the virus you already have.

Q: Can I get HIV if an infected friend gives me a quick kiss?

A: No. Saliva holds only a tiny amount of the virus. If your friend poured a bucket of saliva down your throat, then you should be worried.

Q: Can HIV develop in my body all by itself?

A: No it can't. The only way to get HIV is if it's passed to you from someone who's already infected.

HIV

↘ human immuno-
deficiency virus
↘ AIDS virus

HIV is a virus that lives in human blood. It's not in everyone's blood, just the blood of people who've been infected. This could be anyone, regardless of age, skin colour, sexual orientation, religion, or nationality. Once it's in your blood there's nothing you can do to get it out. But there are many ways you can prevent it from getting there in the first place. See Protection to find out how you can be in control. HIV progresses from an infection to a life-threatening disease, AIDS, in 4 stages.

Stage 1:

This begins just after infection and can last a few weeks. Stage 1 is sometimes marked by an illness that's a lot like the flu, though in 20% of victims, a very nasty flu. An HIV test done at this time may not show you have the virus.

Stage 2:

This is the longest of the 4 stages, lasting up to 10 years. During this time there are almost no symptoms and the person may look and feel perfectly healthy. But the virus is still progressing. Slowly, it's destroying the blood's CD4 cells, which normally exist in large numbers to fight off disease. The fewer CD4 cells you have, the weaker your immune system is and the harder it is to avoid illness. The body fights back at this stage by replacing the lost CD4 cells with as many new ones as possible, but it's always a losing battle. To help in the battle, researchers have developed powerful anti-viral drugs that can be taken by people with HIV. For more about these drugs, see Treatment.

Stage 3:

This stage begins when the body's CD4 cells are overwhelmed by the huge amount of virus that lives in the blood. With the immune system failing, the time is ripe for opportunistic infections to move in. These are infections our bodies usually fight off easily. But now they take hold and symptoms of disease develop. At first these symptoms are mild—fatigue, diarrhoea, yeast infections, fever, weight loss, night sweats, swelling of the lymph glands, mouth infections, a cough that won't go away—but as the immune system erodes, the symptoms worsen.

Stage 4:

When the symptoms of disease (such as tuberculosis or cancer) become very severe, an AIDS diagnosis follows. Even at this point, anti-virals can slow down the progress of HIV.

How you catch it

HIV is present in the blood, ejaculate, and pre-ejaculate of infected males and in the vaginal fluids and menstrual blood of infected females. Because of this, HIV is mainly spread by having unprotected vaginal or anal sex with an infected person. Though the risk is lower, you can also catch it by performing unprotected oral sex—especially by letting a guy come in your mouth or going down on a woman who has her period. Sharing sex toys with someone who has HIV can also lead to infection. To avoid this, clean the toys or change the condom if it's a dildo before exchanging them. Because there's only a minuscule amount of HIV in the saliva of an infected person, you don't have to worry about saliva. HIV can also be transmitted by sharing a hypodermic needle with someone who has the virus, and it can be passed to babies during pregnancy or birth, or through breastfeeding.

2 kinds of testing

1. BLOOD

This is the most available type of testing. Using a needle, a health care worker draws a small amount of blood from your arm. The blood is sent to a laboratory to be checked for antibodies to the virus. When the results come back—in 1 to 2 weeks—you're advised to return to the place where your blood was taken to find out if you're negative or positive. A positive result will usually have been confirmed by a second or third test, though at some private laboratories only one test is done. When more than 1 test is done, the findings are 99.9% accurate.

Many departments of medicine and sexual health clinics now perform rapid HIV tests, which means that you can get your results within 24 hours.

Protect yourself

During intercourse or anal sex, protect yourself by using a condom. If you're having oral sex, use a condom or a dam. To avoid infection, some people put off having intercourse, anal sex, and oral sex until they're in a long-term monogamous relationship.

Getting tested

If there's a chance you've been exposed to HIV, go for testing. A positive result means the test has detected HIV antibodies in your blood. These antibodies can only be present if you have the virus. In other words, HIV antibodies = HIV. Even if your test is negative, it doesn't mean you're HIV-free. Because the virus can be in your bloodstream for up to 3 months before the antibodies show up (in rare cases, 6 months), for accurate results you have to wait 3 months from the time of possible infection to get tested. If you have definitely been exposed to HIV, a further test at 6 months may be advised. While waiting for an HIV test, avoid having unprotected sex (if you've got the virus, you don't want to pass it on). If you have unprotected sex before your results come in and it turns out you're not infected, you'll have to wait 3 months and get tested all over again.

Testing is available through your general practice surgery, or a GU or sexual health clinic. When it comes to HIV testing, most health care professionals will respect your right to privacy, no matter what your age, but you'll feel better having this confirmed. Counselling plus testing takes about half an hour.

2 kinds of testing

2. SALIVA

A test that checks your saliva for antibodies to HIV is called an oral test. It involves opening your mouth and letting a health care worker rub a swab across your gums and on the insides of your cheeks. Your results, which are 99.9% accurate, will be returned to you in 1 to 2 weeks. Because this procedure is new, its availability is limited.

Q & A

Q: Can I get AIDS from taking an HIV test?

A: No. Testing for HIV puts you in no danger at all.

Q & A

Q: What's the difference between anonymous testing and confidential testing?

A: *Anonymous* testing means your name isn't connected to your test. Instead, your test is given a code (and usually a clinic number and date of birth), and this is what appears on the request forms in the lab.

With *confidential* testing, the results of your test are kept in a medical file with your name on it. You can give a false name if you prefer and can choose to withhold details of your G.P. Confidential records are kept separately from other records. Departments of GU medicine and sexual health provide high levels of confidentiality, but if you are worried about who might see your medical records, talk to your G.P. or a member of staff at the clinic.

HIV
Home testing

This is available in some countries (e.g., the United States), but has not yet been approved for use in the U.K.

A positive result

A positive result means you have the virus in your blood for the rest of your life. This can be very difficult to accept. It helps tremendously if you have the support of family and friends. But even the people who love you most may not be able to offer you the information you need to cope with your new situation. This is why it's important to seek the help of a trained counsellor as soon as you get a positive result. He or she will explain treatment options, outline what you can do to avoid spreading the virus, and refer you to a support group. Most counsellors will provide a list of doctors who specialize in HIV. You'll also discuss lifestyle choices that will keep you healthy for as long as possible. The best counselling is face-to-face counselling.

Half of all new HIV infections occur among young people aged 15 to 24.

HIV

Treatment

People with HIV try to keep in excellent shape through rest, good nutrition, and exercise. Their goal is to keep their immune system strong enough to fight off illnesses. Also, drugs have been developed that slow down the spread of HIV in the blood. If the virus spreads slowly, the immune system is able to do its job longer.

These drugs are called anti-virals or "cocktails," and new ones are being discovered all the time. Usually a combination of 3 anti-virals is taken as a kind of insurance. If the virus suddenly changes shape and is no longer vulnerable to one of the drugs, the other 2 will continue to fight until you begin taking a new combination. You and your doctor will decide when the time is right to start taking these drugs—as soon as you test positive or only when your CD4 count falls below a certain number. Because anti-virals are so new, their long-term effectiveness is unknown. How safe they are for users to take over a long period is also unknown.

There is still no cure for HIV.

Heterosexual females are more vulner- able to HIV infection than heterosexual males because of the high concentration of HIV in semen.

It's against the law for a person to be discriminated against or harassed because he or she has HIV or AIDS.

Homogphobia
↘queer fear

This means a fear and hatred of homosexuality and of homosexual individuals. Many people consider feelings of homophobia to be extreme, irrational, and ugly. Certainly, gays, lesbians, and bisexuals think so. This isn't surprising considering they've been the target of so much aggression (gay-bashing) over the years. Gay-bashing includes verbal abuse, physical abuse, and extreme violence that in some cases ends in murder. Sometimes feelings of homophobia are directed more at men than at women. For example, some men hate the idea of gay sex because they feel it threatens their masculinity, while they feel excited by the idea of lesbian sex. Other men, however, feel their masculinity is threatened by lesbian sex because it excludes them, and as a result, these men direct their homophobia at lesbians. Generally, homophobic women don't act out their deep feelings of hatred through physical violence.

Many societies throughout history have accepted some homosexual activity, including those found in a number of Arabic countries, Ancient Greece, and native New Guinea. On the other hand, Europeans, most of whom were of Catholic or Protestant descent, built a Christian society that viewed homosexuality strictly as a sin. Then, for most of the last century, it was considered to be an illness. The result of these attitudes was widespread homophobia, where ignorance and negative stereotypes influenced people to make laws that discriminated against homosexual activity and same-sex couples. Some of these laws still exist today. For example, in the U.K. same-sex couples may have a "partnership

Q & A

Q: How do you know if you're homosexual?

A: You're not necessarily gay or lesbian if you've had same-sex fantasies, masturbated with a group of friends, or experimented sexually a couple of times with someone of your sex. Lots of heterosexuals have done one or all of these things. However, you may be gay or lesbian if your same-sex feelings and fantasies continue month after month, if you're never attracted to someone of the opposite sex, and if you feel different from your heterosexual friends. To know for sure you have to take the plunge and explore the possibilities.

Q: How do gays and lesbians have sex?

A: Homosexual sex is pretty much the same as heterosexual sex minus the penis-vagina penetration. It's made up of kissing, touching, extensive oral sex and mutual masturbation, and sometimes, anal sex.

Q: Can I catch homosexuality?

A: Homosexuality isn't a disease. Neither is heterosexuality. These are different ways that people respond sexually to the people around them.

Coming out

Most people who are heterosexual don't think twice about expressing themselves sexually. Unfortunately, people who are lesbian or gay, or who think they may be, don't have the same luxury. For their safety and security, they often hide their sexual feelings, at least during their teen years. But sooner or later, many lesbians and gays decide it's time to stop hiding who they really are.

Deciding to be open about your sexuality is called "coming out." It means gradually putting the pain of hiding your sexuality behind you. It's a scary process that begins with admitting to yourself that you're gay or lesbian, and then becoming comfortable with the idea. After that, most people come out in stages—first to their most trusted friends, then to their parents, after that to co-workers, and so on. But the order doesn't matter; what matters is coming out with the support of as many people as possible.

For many lesbians and gays, coming out also means learning about sex by experimenting with different partners. This is an important way of confirming sexual identity. However, some people can be so focused on the difficult emotions and challenges of coming out that they forget to use protection. As a result they're at greater risk of catching HIV and other sexually transmitted infections. Using protection makes coming out much safer.

Homophobia

registration ceremony" (so that their union is publicly recognized) or a religious blessing. However, these ceremonies are not legally recognized and confer no rights on the partners.

As an ever-growing number of people realize that homosexuality is a normal sexual response, homophobia has become the target of criticism.

Is our homophobic society to blame for the extremely high suicide rate among young homosexual males? If homophobia suddenly disappeared, what reason would these men have for killing themselves?

Homosexual

This word describes someone who feels romantically and sexually attracted to people of the same sex. Some teenagers are certain about their lesbian or gay orientation at a very young age. Others experiment, usually tentatively, with homosexual feelings and actions and only realize over time that they're truly lesbian or gay (some find out they're heterosexual after all). Accepting who they are and learning to express their sexuality freely can be difficult and take several more years.

Many teens who suspect they're gay or lesbian don't want to face it. Given society's homophobia, it's easy to imagine the confusion, fear, loneliness, low self-esteem, and even self-hatred they sometimes feel. All of this is extremely stressful and painful. Fortunately, most cities have an active, well-organized network of gay and lesbian rights organizations that can help if you or someone you know is struggling with issues of sexuality. Working your way through your feelings and fears can be made incredibly easier by talking to someone who has had positive experiences in this area and is eager to share practical advice. See Resources at the end of the book.

Hormones

These are important chemicals produced by various glands in the body. Once produced, they go straight into the bloodstream. Their purpose is to influence what happens in our bodies and the way we feel. This book is concerned only with the sex hormones.

In females

Female sex hormones are produced primarily in the ovaries. The 2 most important ones are oestrogen and progesterone. Early in the growth of a foetus, oestrogen directs the development of the vulva, uterus, and fallopian tubes. Later, it sets in motion the changes of puberty, helps regulate the menstrual cycle, and prepares the vagina for penetration by making it wet during arousal. Progesterone joins oestrogen in the regulation of the menstrual cycle and also plays a role in preparing the uterine lining for pregnancy.

A woman's adrenal glands produce more oestrogen, as well as some androgens, including testosterone. Testosterone is the hormone that stimulates both the male and female sex drive. Less of it is produced in females than in males, but enough to cause new hair growth at puberty. The sudden appearance of pimples can also be blamed on androgens, which cause glands in the face and back to produce more oils. The production of progesterone after ovulation can also lead to pimples. The same progesterone is what causes vaginal discharge to become clear and slippery for a few days after ovulation.

In males

Male sex hormones are produced in the testicles. The most important group of hormones is called androgens. Of all the androgens, testosterone, which is the hormone behind the male and female sex drive, is the most well-known. Early in the growth of a foetus, testosterone directs the development of the penis and scrotum. Later, it sets in motion the changes of puberty (new hair growth, oily skin, bigger muscles). Males produce more testosterone than females do. A man's adrenal glands make even more androgens, as well as a small amount of the female hormone oestrogen.

Q & A

Q: Why do guys want to have sex more often than girls?

A: Starting in puberty, boys' bodies produce a huge amount of testosterone. This is the hormone that excites the sex drive, in both males and females. Guys have a lot more testosterone than girls do, but that doesn't mean all guys have the same amount. There are guys who don't want sex all the time. But many do, and it's because of all that testosterone.

HPV is the commonest sexually transmitted viral infection in the U.K. It's estimated that 20 to 30% of sexually active young women will contract HPV infection of the cervix at some time. In most cases, this is a fairly short-term infection, with the virus being cleared within 1 to 2 years.

Virginity has nothing to do with whether or not you have a hymen. A virgin is someone who hasn't had sexual intercourse.

Human Papillomavirus
HPV

This isn't one virus, but a family of many different viruses, over 100 different types according to new research. All of these viruses are highly contagious, and it's estimated that many thousands of sexually active people in the United Kingdom are infected with one or more of them. A few HPV strains cause common skin warts, while several others are responsible for genital warts, which are transmitted through sexual contact. Other types of HPV have been closely associated with the development of cancerous cells in the cervix. There's no cure for HPV, though treatments are available that deal with symptoms such as warts and cancerous cells. See Cancer, Genital Warts.

Hymen ♀
cherry

For centuries, through its absence or presence, a young woman's hymen indicated her sexual status. If she had a hymen, she was considered a virgin. As a virgin, she was a valuable commodity that could be sold to a prospective husband for a good price. The future husband would happily pay that price in exchange for knowing that any child she produced would be his. If her hymen was missing, she was considered unacceptable as a bride. Her life was ruined, and in some societies, her family's life was ruined too. In Greek mythology, Hymenaeus (Hymen for short) was the god of marriage.

Hymen

The hymen is actually a small, thin, ordinary piece of skin that only partially covers the opening to the vagina due to the fact that it has one or more holes in it. The holes are necessary to allow menstrual fluid to leave the vagina. Like noses, breasts, toes, and every other part of the human body, hymens differ in size and shape. One girl may have several small holes in a large hymen. Another may have only one big one in a small hymen. Some girls may have 2 or 3 holes of varying proportions, while others are born without a hymen at all. Regardless of size and shape, many hymens are stretched or torn in the course of an active childhood (through activities such as bike riding, tree climbing, or gymnastics) and are long gone by the time of first sex. In modern times, hymens can also be pushed aside by tampon use or a pelvic examination. Depending on the state of your hymen, having sex for the first time will stretch it, tear it, or do nothing at all. Tearing may hurt briefly and result in a small amount of bleeding.

Impotence

Men who have an ongoing problem getting or keeping an erection are classified as suffering from impotence. This condition is uncommon in young men. When impotence does happen at a young age, the cause is usually psychological and can be successfully treated by a therapist. In older men, the problem can still be psychological, although there's a greater chance the cause will be physical. At any age, impotence is sometimes the result of drug use or too much alcohol. Impotence is not the same as failing to get or keep an erection once in a while, which happens to most guys at one time or another. See Erection.

Smokers are twice as likely as non-smokers to become impotent.

Infertility

In females

There are many reasons why a woman might be infertile: her ovaries don't produce eggs; she has endometriosis or hormonal problems; her fallopian tubes are blocked; there's something wrong with her uterus or cervix; or the mucus in her cervix is abnormal.

In males

A man is infertile if he has even one of these problems: his testicles don't produce sperm; he has a low sperm count; his semen has plenty of good sperm, but it's blocked or rerouted and doesn't make it into his penis; or his sperm is abnormal. Infertility can also be caused by the inability to get or keep an erection. Researchers have noticed that every year more and more men have these problems. They speculate that environmental chemicals, among other factors, are to blame. See Ejaculation.

Infertility

The medical definition of infertility is when after 2 years of trying, a man or woman is unable to conceive a child, or the woman is unable to carry the foetus to term. Research shows that infertility strikes about as many men as women. For couples who want children, being infertile can be a difficult, sometimes devastating, situation. See PID.

Around 17% of women treated for pelvic inflammatory disease (which can develop if a chlamydia infection isn't treated) will become infertile.

Intimacy

Intimacy is when 2 people share a very close, personal relationship. You probably have a relationship like this in your life. It could be with your mother, father, sister, brother, or other relative. It could be with a friend or neighbour, or a boyfriend or girlfriend. It's possible to be intimate with many people at once, though each intimate relationship will be different. For example, you may not reveal the same things to your mother that you would to a best friend, and vice versa.

When people you're close with think that intimacy means they can intrude on your personal space—by disrespecting your views or decisions or trying to control your behaviour—it can be irritating or even abusive. But when

Q & A

Q: Is it wrong to want to be with my girlfriend all the time?

A: It's normal to want to spend every waking minute with the person you love, but that doesn't mean it's healthy. You should always save time for yourself, to pursue activities that make you feel good, to develop other friendships, and just to think about what's going on in your life. The better you know yourself—what you like and don't like, what you think about things—the more strength you bring to your relationship and the better it will be.

Q: In relationships, why don't guys talk about their feelings as much as girls do?

A: It's common for many girls to want to share their feelings with their boyfriends early in the relationship. Right from the start, they're ready to be emotionally intimate. But many guys approach intimacy from a different direction— they start by being sexually intimate, and it's only over time that they're able to put their emotions into words. Even then, they may say little. No one knows exactly what's behind these differences. Are they due to the fact that girls are encouraged from an early age to express their feelings? Are guys biologically programmed not to need to talk about their emotions? Most researchers agree that learned social interactions and biology both play a part in how girls and guys respond to each other in relationships.

Intimacy

intimacy is coupled with respect, it can be one of the most enjoyable aspects of a relationship. This kind of intimacy allows you to share your private self by saying what you think and telling your dreams. If your relationship is with a boyfriend or girlfriend, you can feel comfortable admitting what you want and don't want and showing your desire. You can also feel confident (most of the time) that your partner accepts the full range of your personality, the strengths AND weaknesses. This kind of intimacy usually takes time to develop. For it to truly exist, your partner has to feel as comfortable and confident as you do, or close to it. When 2 people don't want the same level of intimacy, their relationship may be headed for trouble.

IUD Advantages

Very effective at stopping pregnancy. Doesn't interfere with sex. Is extremely easy to use (after insertion, there's nothing to do except check every now and again to see if the string is in place). Is inexpensive. Can be left in for several years. There's no mess.

Disadvantages

Doesn't protect against sexually transmitted infections. Can increase your chances of developing pelvic inflammatory disease, which can be painful and lead to sterility. Insertion can cause cramping or bleeding for a few hours or a day.

IUD

↘ coil
↘ intrauterine device

A form of birth control, an IUD is a small piece of plastic wrapped in copper that's inserted into the uterus by a doctor. A short string to remove the IUD is left hanging out of the os (removal must also be performed by a doctor). Of the 2 kinds of IUDs, the Copper-T is more popular. It functions by disrupting the uterus and making it difficult for sperm to reach their target. As well, the copper itself acts as a spermicide. Copper-Ts can be left in for up to 10 years.

Doctors don't usually recommend IUDs for use in teenagers. This is because an IUD can make it easier for infections such as gonorrhoea and chlamydia to move from the cervix into the uterus and fallopian tubes. When this happens, pelvic inflammatory disease may develop, and the result could be sterility. The ideal candidate for an IUD is someone in a monogamous relationship with a partner who is free of chlamydia, gonorrhoea, and other infections.

Keeper ♀

Most girls use sanitary pads or tampons during their period, but there's a relatively new device on the market for collecting menstrual flow. It's called the Keeper. Made of natural gum rubber, the handle and small, flexible cup measure about 7 cm long, though for comfort, it's advised to cut most of the handle off. The Keeper fits snugly in the vagina, where it catches menstrual flow as it drips through the cervix. It holds about 30 ml of liquid at a time (the average period is between 30 and 80 ml in total), and doesn't interfere with urination.

Advocates like the Keeper because it's safe—it's made of a harmless natural product, and it catches your flow rather than soaking it in and possibly drying out the vagina, which is the danger with tampons. It's also environmentally friendly—no trees are cut down to make it, and it's not manufactured in the billions to be thrown away after each use. Used over time, it's much less expensive than either tampons or pads. Also, the Keeper remains effective even during intense physical activity, including swimming. Problems include difficulty with insertion and occasional leaking. Creating a good seal takes practice, as does removing it without spilling the contents.

Labia Majora

This part of the vulva is also known as the outer lips. These 2 spongy flaps of skin protect a woman's inside genital area and are sensitive to touch. By late puberty the outer lips are covered with pubic hair. See Vulva.

Labia Minora

Known as the inner lips, the labia minora are found just inside the outer lips of the vulva. These 2 thinner and hairless flaps of skin are softer than the outer lips and are sometimes wrinkled and dark. In some women they protrude from the outer lips. The labia minora are very sensitive to touch and become swollen and darker in colour when a woman is sexually excited. The shape and size can vary a lot from girl to girl and woman to woman. See Vulva.

Availability

The Keeper can be ordered on the Internet from sites such as www.ecozone.co.uk and www.menses.co.uk. It costs about £30.

Q: Can I wear the Keeper ♀ overnight?

A: Lying down can sometimes break the seal, which results in leakage. If this happens to you, wear a pad while you sleep. Many people have no problem with nighttime use, except, perhaps, that they need to empty the cup partway through the night.

Lesbian

In the 7th century BC, the great poet Sappho wrote beautiful poems of love and adoration to the young women in her life. Many members of her community celebrated these poems and revered her art. Some historians have suggested that Sappho's exalted status indicates that in those times, female homosexuality was an accepted expression of love. Whether this is true or not, the word "lesbian" was taken from Lesbos, the name of Sappho's Greek island homeland. After Sappho's time, same-sex female love fell into serious disrepute and for hundreds of years was one of the great sexual taboos. Today, however, in virtually all big Western cities, lesbian culture—multi-faceted, politically active, and well-organized—is thriving once again. And in towns of every size, many women are part of loving, trusting, long-term relationships with other women.

Love Bite

↘hickey

If your partner sucks on your skin hard enough during sex play (usually on the neck), blood vessels will break and a bruise will appear on the spot that was sucked. This is a love bite. Some people say that lovers give love bites to their partners as a way of marking their territory, of proclaiming, "you belong to me." Others say that a love bite doesn't mean anything, except that the person who gave it was really turned on. What do you think? It takes about 2 weeks for a love bite to go away completely.

Lubrication

Lubrication is hard to achieve for girls who are nervous or reluctant about having sex, worried that it won't feel good, scared of getting pregnant, very tired, hurried through sex, or are in any way distracted from the pleasures of becoming aroused. In some cases, the problem is that the boyfriend doesn't know how to arouse his girlfriend and is afraid to ask. Or maybe he tries to penetrate too soon, before she's had time to get wet. At this point, it's still not too late for the girl to tell her boyfriend what she likes and dislikes. Good communication is essential. If communication is clear and all the distractions have been resolved and the vagina is still dry, the problem can be solved with a tube of store-bought, water-based lubrication, such as K-Y jelly. Manufactured lubrication is safe and does the job just as well as natural secretions.

Lubricants

↘lube

Lubricants are a wonderful sex aid when the vagina is stingy with its own lubrication. This can happen even if the girl feels totally ready in her mind for sex—sometimes the body doesn't cooperate (though if she's not lubricating, she may want to ask herself if she really wants to be penetrated). When the vagina is "dry," the penis isn't able to slide easily in and out, and the girl will feel pain or discomfort. To fix this, a water-based lubricant can be smeared straight onto the condom and added to the vagina as needed. If the activity is anal sex, using a lube is absolutely necessary. Lubricants can also come in handy during fingering.

Only water-based lubricants can be used with latex products such as male condoms, diaphragms, cervical caps, and gloves. Oil-based products cause latex to deteriorate, with the result that germs or sperm can get through. A popular choice is K-Y jelly, which can be found in most chemists, along with other brands. Petroleum-based lubricants can only be used with the female condom or other polyurethane products.

Lubrication

There's no way a woman can enjoy intercourse if her vagina isn't lubricated. For a penis to glide in and out smoothly, or even to enter in the first place, she has to be good and wet. Most of the time, lubrication happens naturally when a woman becomes aroused—her vagina produces secretions that make it wet and slippery. This can happen instantly, though usually it takes a while, up to 20 minutes or longer. But it won't happen if all the conditions of sex aren't right.

Having a lot of hair on your body doesn't mean you're more "masculine" than other guys. If you're hairy, it's because your ancestors were hairy. You inherited their genes.

Masculine

This word describes characteristics and behaviours—mostly good—that are traditionally associated with being male. They include assertiveness, independence, strength of mind, confidence, intelligence, and an ability to take charge. Being male is also associated with acting logically and reasonably, and being unemotional, aggressive, judgmental, and sex crazy. Together, these characteristics and behaviours make up a masculine stereotype that has mostly benefited men for hundreds of years. For example, men who identify with the stereotype and act out its behaviours generally have a better chance of succeeding in the workplace. Many men, however, are intimidated by the stereotype (for example, they often don't feel capable of being assertive or in charge). Others are frustrated by the limited range of behaviours that expectations of "manliness" allow. They'd like to be able to express an interest, say, in home or relationships, without having people question their masculinity. In terms of sex, men who are comfortable with the so-called masculine characteristics of confidence and assertiveness are initiators in bed, and generally enjoy their experiences. Men who are also thoughtful and willing to please—2 of the so-called feminine characteristics—often have deeper, more fulfilling relationships, as well as improved sex lives.

See Feminine.

Masturbation

↘wanking
↘playing with
   yourself
↘jacking off
↘bashing the bishop
↘jerking off
↘whacking off
↘self-pleasuring

Masturbation is an ancient practice. For thousands of years individuals felt physical desire and touched their genitals. If they touched them in just the right way and for just the right amount of time, they reached orgasm. Their sexual tension was released and they felt good. Then, in some parts of the world, people began to discourage masturbation, fearing that it wasted precious life-giving semen. Elsewhere, other groups developed the religious idea that the sole purpose of sexual activity was procreation. Soon masturbation was considered to be a great evil. By the 1800s, scientific papers were being published that described how masturbation drained the body of vital fluids, ruining good health. The supposed consequences included acne, headaches, baldness, blindness, memory loss, insanity, sterility, epilepsy, weak limbs, and even hairy palms. In fact, publicizing these risks was simply a scare tactic meant to discourage people from masturbating. Today, it's been proven that masturbation causes no ill effects and is in fact a normal and healthy sexual activity.

Reasons to masturbate

↘It feels good
↘You learn about your body
↘You learn about your sexual response
↘It releases sexual tension
↘There's no risk of pregnancy
↘There's no risk of sexually transmitted infections
↘You can be sexual without having a partner

Q & A

Q: If I don't climax, does it mean I'm not really masturbating?

A: If you're giving yourself sexual pleasure with your hands or an object, you're masturbating—whether or not you climax.

Q: Do guys stop growing if they masturbate too much? ♂

A: No matter how often you masturbate, you'll grow as tall as you were destined to grow. Masturbation won't bend your penis, make it smaller, or negatively affect your body in any way.

Females do it

In recent surveys more females than ever say they masturbate. Is this because there are actually more women masturbating or because women are starting to feel comfortable admitting it? Probably both. Regardless of the statistics, women of all ages give themselves sexual pleasure in a variety of ways: by using their fingers to stroke the vulva and clitoris, by putting a finger or fingers in the vagina, by stimulating the vulva with a vibrator or a jet of water from a shower head, by pushing against a pillow, or by rhythmically pressing their legs together. It's not unusual for women to use their free hand to stroke their breasts or other erogenous zones. Some women fantasize as they masturbate, while others think of nothing at all, preferring to focus on the sensations.

Males do it

Over 90% of guys masturbate, either a little or a lot. The usual method is to hold the shaft of the penis in one hand, then to move the hand up and down rhythmically and with varying degrees of pressure. This will eventually lead to ejaculation and orgasm. For some guys, the pleasure is increased by stroking their glans or scrotum with their free hand, or by using lubrication (saliva or a commercial lubricant such as K-Y jelly) to reduce the friction. Another way to masturbate is to pump the penis between 2 pillows or to rub it against a mattress. Usually, masturbation goes hand in hand with fantasizing. Some guys like to do it while looking at sexy magazines or Internet images or watching erotic films. Others just like to think about someone who turns them on. For many guys, masturbation is an excellent way to learn how to control the timing of their ejaculations.

Q & A

Q: I tried masturbating once but my vagina was dry and I didn't feel anything. Should I keep trying?

A: Only keep trying if you're interested in exploring new sensations. If you are, using a lubricant will make masturbating easier until your own lubrication kicks in. But that may not happen the first time you masturbate, or even the second or third time. Becoming good at masturbating takes practice, so be patient. Some people feel uneasy or guilty about masturbating. If that's true for you, it's okay not to do it.

Q: Can I become infected with HIV from masturbating?

A: Masturbating doesn't lead to HIV or any other sexually transmitted infection. To become infected, you must have contact with someone who already has the infection.

Q: Do girls masturbate as much as guys?

A: Not as much, though the gap is closing. After centuries of having to suppress their sexuality, women are increasingly taking control of their sex lives.

During intercourse

No matter how expertly a penis thrusts into a vagina, there's a very good chance the woman won't orgasm. This is because thrusting often doesn't bring the penis into direct contact with the clitoris. What's needed is direct clitoral stimulation, which the woman can provide with her own hand. There are 2 positions that give her easy access to her clitoris during thrusting—woman-on-top or rear entry (doing it "doggy style"). Another way a woman can reach orgasm is by encouraging her partner to stroke her clitoris during thrusting, or by masturbating herself with the tip of his penis in between thrusts. In cases where the man comes before his partner does, a nice way to end the lovemaking is for the man to masturbate her until she comes.

Mutual masturbation

This is a big, wonderful part of lesbian and gay sex, and a perfect alternative to intercourse for many heterosexual couples. During mutual masturbation, partners use their hands, or an object such as a dildo or vibrator, to excite each other's genitals. Continued excitement leads to full arousal, which often leads to orgasm. Through mutual masturbation, couples can watch each other's responses and learn a lot about what's pleasurable to their partner and what isn't. It's also an excellent time to ask questions and explore new techniques. Some partners enjoy the excitement of masturbating each other simultaneously.

Q & A

Q: Now that I have a boyfriend, should I stop masturbating?

A: Sex with a partner and masturbation are 2 different experiences with unique sensations. It's possible, and even healthy, to enjoy both in the context of a good relationship. In fact, because both partners in a couple may not have the same sex drive, masturbation allows one to enjoy sex during those times when the other isn't "in the mood." Some couples find it a turn-on to watch each other masturbate. Will it bother your boyfriend if you continue to masturbate from time to time? Some people are afraid that if their partner masturbates, it means he or she doesn't find them sexually attractive. If this is how your boyfriend feels, you should talk about it.

Mutual Masturbation Protection

STIs such as herpes and genital warts can be transmitted during mutual masturbation if your partner is infected and you don't wash your hands before touching your own body. Transmitting HIV through semen or vaginal secretions is possible if one or both partners have open cuts or sores on their hands. To decrease the risk, you can use latex gloves, condoms, or non-microwavable plastic wrap.

Q: Should I be worried
if I don't have my
period at 16?

A: Some girls only get their
period at 16. But if you're
17 and you don't have it,
you should see a doctor
to find out if you have
primary amenorrhoea,
which is the failure to
start menstruating at
puberty. This frequently
happens with athletes or
dancers who train intensely.
Gaining weight and improving
your diet may be all that's
needed to get your period
started.

Q: Do men suffer from
a male version of
menopause?

A: Some people think so
and have even given it a
name: andropause. To
find out if andropause
really exists, researchers
are conducting studies on
middle-aged men with low
levels of testosterone.
The jury is still out.

Menarche ♀

Getting your first period is called menarche
(pronounced muh-NAR-key). In some girls it
happens very early, at 8 or 9 years old, or it can
happen as late as 16. Most girls get their first period
between 11 and 14. Menarche is a sign that you may
be able to get pregnant.

If your period hasn't started yet, you can
roughly predict its arrival by thinking back to when
your breasts first started developing. Menarche
should happen about 2 years after that, or about
1 year after your first pubic hairs show up. Or ask
your mother and grandmothers when they started
menstruating; because menarche is partly hereditary,
you could begin at around the same time. Once
your period starts, you'll get it every month for
the next 40 or 45 years, except if you're pregnant
or breastfeeding.

Menopause

A woman experiences menopause on the day her
last-ever menstrual cycle ends. At this point, she is
no longer able to get pregnant. In most women this
happens between the ages of 45 and 55. Menopause
is preceded by several years of perimenopause, which
is when the body produces less and less oestrogen.
Perimenopause is marked by irregular periods and
emotional ups and downs. Most women can expect
to have about 500 periods in their lifetime.

Menstrual Cycle ♀

A woman's pattern of menstruation is called her menstrual cycle. On average, it goes like this: the first day of your period marks the first day of your cycle. For the next 13 days an egg matures in one of your 2 ovaries (alternating ovaries every month). At the same time, the lining of the uterus grows thicker in case a fertilized egg needs to lodge there. On day 14 the egg is released into the fallopian tube, an important event called ovulation. Now the egg has to travel through the fallopian tube to the uterus, which takes a couple of days. If the egg isn't fertilized during its travels, it disintegrates and flows out the vagina. At this point the lining of the uterus starts to break down because it isn't needed after all. Several days later your period starts: the old lining has to be cast off to make room for a new lining to grow in case the next egg gets fertilized. The last day before your period starts is the last day of your cycle. After first menstruation, it can take a year or 2 before your cycle becomes regular.

The average cycle is 28 days long, which means that it's 28 days from the first day of your period to the day before the first day of your next period. A girl with a 28-day cycle can say it's "regular" when it's 28 days every time, though it's not uncommon for the length of your cycle to vary slightly from month to month. Many girls have short cycles (21 days) or long ones (35 days), or anywhere in between. Just because your cycle is regular for years (say, 26 days) doesn't mean it won't change all of a sudden. There are several factors that can influence the length of your cycle, including nutrition, weight change, stress, and travel. Regardless of how long your menstrual cycle is, ovulation almost always happens 14 days before the beginning of your next period.

Q & A ♀

Q: Can I know ahead of time when I'm going to ovulate?

A: If your cycle is regular and you know how long it is, it's easy to figure out when your next ovulation date will be. Just determine when the first day of your next period will be, then count back 14 days. For example, if your last period started on June 1 and your cycle is usually 25 days long, then your next period will start on June 26. Count back 14 days to June 12. That's your ovulation date. If you don't have sex for 9 days around this date (4 days before; 4 after), you'll lower your risk of getting pregnant. It won't eliminate the risk completely because you can never be 100% sure when you'll ovulate. Couples who try to avoid pregnancy by timing their intercourse to these calculations have a 20% failure rate. That's a lot of failure! Put another way, if this is the only protection you use, you can expect to become pregnant within a year. See Rhythm Method.

Menstruation ♀
↘menses
↘your period

Once a month, beginning in puberty, the female body rids itself of the lining of the uterus. Women refer to this event as their "period." Menstruation usually lasts between 2 and 6 days, though it can be over in a day or hang around for up to 8 days. The amount of fluid lost is usually about 30 to 80 ml, but this can vary from month to month. Pregnant women don't menstruate because the embryo needs the uterine lining as a bed and for nutrition. See Menarche, Menstrual Cycle, Period Pains, PMS.

Problems

Most periods are regular and normal, but once in a while something can go wrong. Ask a doctor to check you out if you experience any of the following: your period pains are so bad that they keep you in bed, or they go on for more than 3 days; your bleeding is so heavy that you can't keep up with the flow, no matter how often you change your tampon or pad (a half day of this might be normal; a day or more isn't); your period is still going strong after 7 days; you're past the second-year mark and your periods are still irregular (shorter than 21 days or longer than 35 days for 3 periods in a row); you bleed lightly between periods (called spotting).

Sometimes girls stop getting their period even though they're not pregnant. This condition is called secondary amenorrhoea, and usually it's nothing serious. Having your period stop can be a sign that you're suffering from physical or emotional stress. It's your body's way of telling you it feels overexerted. This can happen if you're exercising heavily (training as a track athlete, dancer, figure skater, or gymnast), if you've been travelling a lot, if you're suffering from extreme anxiety, if you've gained or lost a lot of weight, or if you're taking certain drugs. See a doctor to find out what you can do to return to a healthy menstrual cycle.

Secondary amenorrhoea can also be a symptom of anorexia nervosa or bulimia. When severely underfed or malnourished, the body senses that it can't support a foetus and will break from its usual menstrual cycle. If this is the case, it's crucial that you get help immediately. Anorexia and bulimia can lead to serious health complications or even death. See a doctor and ask for appropriate therapy.

Almost everyone thinks of menstrual fluid as blood, but in fact it's mostly tissue and mucus, with some blood mixed in.

Miscarriage
↘spontaneous abortion

Ten to 20 per cent of pregnancies end in miscarriage, which is when a woman's body rejects the embryo (or foetus) that's growing inside it. If this happens very early, the miscarriage may not even be noticed. When it happens later, the woman will experience various degrees of abdominal pain and bleeding, depending on the age of the foetus. Many miscarriages occur when fertilized eggs don't implant correctly and are expelled in the first 2 to 3 months of pregnancy. Other embryos abort due to abnormalities. Because expectant parents fall in love with their developing babies and build dreams around them, a miscarriage can cause psychological and emotional pain.

Q: If I have molluscum
contagiosum bumps,
how long will I
be contagious?

A: As long as you have
the bumps, you're
contagious. When
every last bump is
gone, you no longer
have to worry about
giving the virus to
someone else.

Molluscum Contagiosum

This skin infection is caused by a virus. If you've caught it, you won't know for several weeks or even months. Then one day, what look like small pimples will appear on your skin. Soon they become shiny, flesh-coloured bumps. The centre of each bump is slightly depressed and holds a tiny amount of soft, white pus. There's no itching, though some of the bumps may become red and slightly sore. Many people mistake the bumps for genital warts.

Molluscum contagiosum bumps can develop anywhere on your body, but if you've caught the virus because you've had sex with an infected partner, they'll probably show up on your genitals, buttocks, or thighs. You may have 10 or 20 of them, or even up to 100. They're easily transmitted from one area of the body to another if skin-to-skin contact is frequent. Children often share the virus with friends and siblings through casual touching. It can also be spread in swimming pools.

Testing

One look at the bumps and a doctor should be able to tell you what they are. Some doctors may scrape away the centre of a bump and study it under a microscope to be certain of their diagnosis.

Treatment

The only treatment is to remove the soft centres. When this is done, the bumps will eventually disappear. Unfortunately, as some bumps disappear, others will pop up as a result of self-infection. Sometimes it can take a few years before all the bumps are gone. Because of the danger of self-infection, it's best to treat the bumps while they are still few in number. If the bumps come back, try to treat them as soon as possible. There are no long-term health consequences to molluscum contagiosum.

Prevention

Don't have direct contact, sexual or otherwise, with someone who has molluscum contagiosum bumps. If you want to have sex, not even a condom can fully protect you.

Monogamy

This is about sticking to one boyfriend or girlfriend for a long time in a serious, loving, sexual relationship. (This doesn't mean you have to have sex with your partner; you just have to share a sexual attraction.) This kind of relationship usually has a high level of trust, enjoyment, and intimacy. Being comfortable with each other's feelings about sex is important too. A serious breakdown in any of these areas will probably end with the couple splitting up. Serial monogamy is when you have one sexual relationship at a time, many times in a row.

A sexually active couple has to be monogamous for at least 6 months, and have tested negative for all sexually transmitted infections at the 6-month mark, before they can even think about dropping barrier methods from their sex and using only birth control. The problem is, it's impossible to test for some STIs when there are no symptoms, and some symptoms take longer than 6 months to surface. For example, the symptoms of herpes and genital warts may not show up for a year, and a person could still be contagious in the interim. Also, it's possible one of the partners has been unfaithful (either before the 6-month mark or following testing) and is carrying germs. To be as safe as possible, use a condom.

Q & A

Q: Do people sometimes die from mono?

A: Never. Mono always goes away over time.

Mononucleosis

↘ **mono**

↘ **the kissing disease**

People call mono the kissing disease because it's caused by a virus that's spread when saliva is exchanged. It's possible to get it from sharing a toothbrush, utensils, or a cup with someone who's infected, but it's very unlikely that you'll catch it in these ways. This is because mono isn't highly contagious. If you become infected with mono, it's probably because you're already overtired and your immune system is weak. Once you have it, your body becomes so exhausted that it doesn't want to do anything. Other symptoms you can detect include headaches, fever, sore throat, swelling of the lymph glands in your neck, and in some cases, a skin rash.

Treatment

If you have mono, all you can do is eat nutritious foods and get lots of rest. Your body will tell you when it's ready to be active again. Some people are back on their feet in a week, while it can take up to a month or more for others to feel their normal energy return.

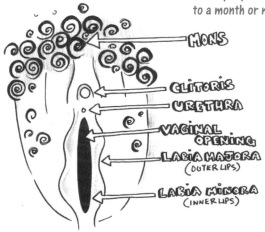

MONS

CLITORIS

URETHRA

VAGINAL OPENING

LABIA MAJORA (OUTER LIPS)

LABIA MINORA (INNER LIPS)

Mons

↘ pubis

This is the soft area just over the female pubic bone where pubic hair grows. It's also known as the Mound of Venus (in Greek mythology Venus is the goddess of love). Sometimes pressing the mons creates sexual excitement.

Multiple Partners

Three people getting together to have sex is called a ménage à trois or threesome. This is the stuff of fantasy, especially for some guys (fantasizing about being with 2 girls is a way of confirming their masculinity). But many people say that threesomes are rarely as much fun in real life as they are in dreamland. According to one 21-year-old, "Threesomes really aren't all they're cracked up to be. There are too many hands and legs and tongues. You're always thinking, 'Am I paying too much attention to this person? Is the other one jealous? Are they paying enough attention to me?' "

Threesomes can be nerve-wracking in other ways too. For example, now you have to sexually satisfy 2 people, not just 1, and if you're a guy and the third person is a guy, does that mean you're gay? Are you a lesbian if you're female and you're with a guy and a girl? Where do emotions fit in? Are you getting what you want from the encounter? Despite the potential for discomfort and confusion, many people are still interested in trying a threesome, at least once. Of those who try it, some will enter into it strictly as sexual play and will enjoy themselves.

When more than 3 people get together to have sex, it's called group sex or an orgy. This is about bodies coming together, not about relationships or emotions. The more bodies there are, the greater your chances of contracting a sexually transmitted infection. Birth control, condoms, and dams should be used, but with so much going on at once, it's easy for protection to be forgotten. People who engage in a ménage à trois also run a greater risk of catching an infection, or more than one. Multiple partners also refers to having more than one sex partner, but not in the same bed all at once.

Q: How can I tell my girlfriend that I don't want to try a threesome?

A: Threesomes can be difficult for couples, even when both partners agree they want to try it. Feelings of jealousy can spring up unexpectedly, and it's not uncommon that somewhere along the line, trust is broken. Even if the encounter ends pleasantly, new insecurities can fester. Even the most secure, mature couples risk disrupting their relationship if they engage in a threesome. Tell your feelings honestly to your girlfriend. In a good relationship, no one has to do anything that makes them feel uncomfortable.

Nipples

Female nipples get a lot more attention than male ones, probably because they're attached to female breasts. But what most of us think of as the nipple—the pink or peach or tan or dark brown area of skin that crowns the breast—is actually the areola. At the tip of the areola is the nipple.

In females ♀

There is variety in nipples. Some are slightly pointed, some are round or flat. Protruding nipples can protrude a lot or a little. Nipples that are turned in instead of sticking out are called inverted nipples and aren't as uncommon as you think. If you have inverted nipples, it's possible they'll turn out before your breasts finish growing. If they don't, don't worry. You can still enjoy sex and you'll still be able to breastfeed a baby one day. Nipples that turn in suddenly, however, may indicate a problem and should be checked by a doctor.

If you look closely, you'll see a few small openings in the ends of your nipples. Those are the ducts where milk will come out should you ever give birth. But even when pregnancy is the last thing on your mind, it's possible to have a bit of milk-like fluid discharge from your nipples every now and again. This is normal and nothing to worry about. Women on the Pill may have discharge from their nipples more frequently. If the discharge continues for more than a week, see a doctor to find out if there's a problem. If you have inverted nipples, discharge can collect in the folds of your areolae, so wash there regularly to avoid infection.

The nipple and areola are the most sensitive parts of the breast. This doesn't mean every woman likes to be touched there, just most women! Arousal makes nipples get hard and stick straight out, and bumps pop up on the areola. The same things happen when you suddenly get chilly. Sometimes nipples can feel too sensitive, like when they're very dry or you don't wear a bra and a rough fabric rubs against them once too often. If this happens, put on a bra until the sensitivity passes and treat your nipples to a bit of lanolin (a product made from the oil found on sheep's wool) or another soothing ointment.

♂ In males

Guys' nipples are just like girls' nipples in many ways: they look about the same (though most girls have much bigger areolae), they're filled with nerve endings and are sensitive to touch, they contract during sexual excitement or cold, they can get sore from rubbing against the rough fabric of a shirt, and they even have milk ducts. Like girls' nipples, guys' nipples deserve to be looked after. They also appreciate attention during lovemaking (though not all guys would agree; ask first if you want to play with his nipples).

Q & A

Q: Am I weird because my areolae are huge? ♀

A: In some girls, the dark covers most of the breast; in others, it's no bigger than a 2p piece. No matter how big or small your areolae, they're as normal as every other part of your body.

Normal

Every day and night—at the cinema, sitting in front of the TV, walking past a magazine rack, checking out the billboards—we are bombarded with images of "perfect" bodies and "perfect" sexual experiences. As a result, people begin to question the legitimacy of their own bodies and experiences. Guys look at their penis and pectorals and wonder if they're good enough. Girls look at their breasts and waistline and wonder how they can make improvements. Faced with new sexual experiences, both girls and guys are convinced they're not normal. Wrong. If they stopped looking at manufactured images for a minute and refocused their gaze on the real, every-day people around them, they would notice that human bodies and body parts come in an amazing and endlessly interesting variety of shapes, colours, and sizes. The same is true of human emotions, thoughts, desires, and behaviours. What's "normal" is for people to be different from each other. Individuals only start to feel normal when they accept the ways they're different. It helps when others around them accept their differences too.

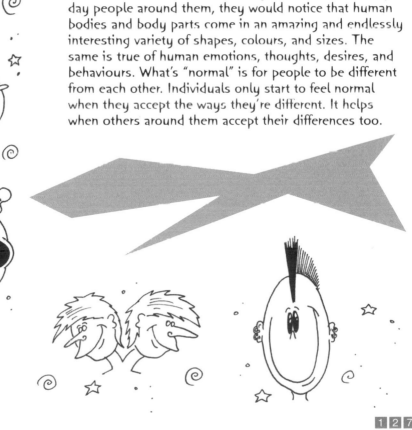

Q&A

Q: What's 69?

A: See how the 9 looks like an upside down 6? When 2 people lie together in this position—head to toe and toe to head—they can give each other oral sex at the same time. Some people really like this position as it stimulates many senses all at once, which can be very exciting. Others find that if you're focusing on giving oral sex, you can't really let loose and enjoy the sensations of receiving it.

Q: Why do guys put their hands on your head when you're giving them a blow job?

A: Maybe they don't realize they're doing it. If their hands are controlling your movements in a way that makes you feel uncomfortable (holding your head steady so they can push their penis in farther than you want it to go, or making you stay still while they ejaculate when you don't want semen in your mouth) tell them you prefer not having their hands there. One of the nice things about giving head is that you control the show.

Oral Sex
↘fellatio
↘cunnilingus
↘going down on
↘giving head
↘eating out

Some people really enjoy giving pleasure by kissing, licking, or sucking their partner's genitals. They like the smell, taste, look, and feel of them, and are intensely turned on by the experience. This is called giving oral sex. Receiving oral sex is when you're the one being stimulated, and for many people, this is even more exciting and sensational than intercourse. There are two kinds of oral sex: fellatio, when your mouth gives pleasure to his penis, and cunnilingus, when your mouth gives pleasure to her vulva.

Oral Sex

Oral sex always involves an exchange of body fluids. In cunnilingus, saliva and vaginal secretions are exchanged, as well as blood if the woman has her period. In fellatio, saliva and semen or pre-ejaculate are exchanged (even if the guy doesn't come in your mouth, a small amount of pre-ejaculate may end up there before he pulls out).

Protection

Because body fluids are exchanged during unprotected oral sex, it's possible for participants to become infected with HIV. Performing fellatio is risky if you have cuts or open sores in your mouth (semen and pre-ejaculate carry the virus in significant amounts). Performing cunnilingus is less risky, unless the woman has her period, when the risk goes up due to the presence of blood. Oral sex also puts you at risk for other sexually transmitted infections.

Where there's a chance of infection, there's need for protection. To keep yourself safe from HIV and some STIs, use a condom during fellatio and a dam during cunnilingus. Unfortunately, using a condom or dam won't fully protect you from herpes or genital warts. If you have numerous partners and fail to practise safer sex in every instance, it's essential to see a doctor and get tested once every 6 months to see if you've caught anything. Many STIs are easily cured if you treat them in the early stages. If you don't treat them, some can turn nasty, leading to serious problems such as infertility, brain damage, and even death. **See Condoms, Dam, Testing.**

Q & A

Q: How can I tell my boyfriend I don't want him to kiss me after he's gone down on me?

A: Pick your timing and tell him as nicely as possible. If you think you can make him laugh, try being funny. Communicating what you like and don't like is an important part of being ready for sex. Not kissing after oral sex is no big deal. There's lots of other stuff that can be enjoyed instead.

As long as both partners keep their genitals clean, there's nothing dirty about oral sex.

Q: Is it true that every woman has faked an orgasm at least once?

A: Surveys report that most women have faked it, but not all. Though the reasons for faking may be good ones—your partner is trying hard to please you and you don't want to disappoint, you're tired and want sex to be over—being dishonest can get you into trouble. If your partner thinks you're climaxing and you're not, he or she will never do anything differently, and you'll be left feeling frustrated. To create a sex life where both you and your partner are satisfied, you have to communicate with each other and work toward getting it right.

Q: Do guys ever fake orgasm?

A: Yes, though not as often as girls do. Here are some reasons that guys fake it: he's too tired to finish what got started; he wasn't interested in sex in the first place; he noticed his erection was dying and wanted to avoid explaining why; he ejaculated without coming and didn't want to admit it.

Orgasm

↘coming ↘cumming
↘climaxing
↘getting off

Intense sexual excitement and continued stimulation of the genitals often lead to orgasm. This is a series of uncontrollable muscle spasms that release sexual tension and cause ripples, waves, or charges of pleasure to radiate or sweep over your body. The intensity of your climax can vary greatly depending on your mood, the source of stimulation, your relationship with your partner, or even the location of your lovemaking.

Everyone responds to orgasms differently. Some people moan or cry out as they orgasm, others remain silent. Some people become fidgety, others lie very still. All these responses are normal. In both sexes, orgasms usually last 5 to 10 seconds and lead to deep feelings of peace and serenity. Female orgasms generally last a bit longer than male ones. Unlike in the movies, partners rarely orgasm at the same time. See Arousal, Ejaculation.

In females

The easiest way for most women to reach orgasm is if their clitoris or the surrounding area is directly stimulated using a finger or tongue. Climaxing is rarer during intercourse because the clitoris receives little or no direct stimulation. Lots of girls don't know much about climaxing because they haven't explored how their bodies can give them pleasure. As a result, they can't tell their partners what feels good. Also, they don't know that it's normal to take a long time to reach orgasm and may feel inadequate if it doesn't happen in 5 or 10 minutes.

Orgasm

If you want to improve your chances of climaxing there are 3 things you can do: discover your anatomy with the help of a mirror, use masturbation to explore how you feel as you become aroused and climax, and experiment with a willing and generous partner. While exploring your body, you may as well check out your G-spot. According to many women, rubbing the G-spot can lead to very nice vaginal orgasms. Studies show that women who know their bodies well have much happier and healthier sex lives.
See Clitoris, G-spot, Vagina.

Multiple orgasms

Most women are capable of multiple orgasms—when the first orgasm is quickly followed by one or more orgasms—if their clitoris continues to receive stimulation, usually by their own hand or by the hand of their partner. Many women, however, are satisfied to stop at one, and some are content not to climax at all.

In males ♂

For most guys it's easy to reach orgasm during intercourse because the penis receives constant direct stimulation. Also, just about everyone with a penis is familiar with the pleasures it can give them thanks to their frequent handling of it, either to urinate, masturbate, or just move it around. Consequently, they have a good idea of what to do to have an orgasm. However, contrary to popular belief, having an orgasm doesn't always occur at the same time as ejaculation. It can happen a bit before or not at all. Ejaculating without climaxing is rare, but when it happens, it can be a letdown.

Multiple orgasms

Not much is known about this phenomenon, except that it exists. Some men are able to feel several small orgasms before the larger one that occurs at the same time as ejaculation. Or they feel one long, intense orgasm for several minutes before ejaculating. Rarely, men have reported being able to come a second time after ejaculating.

A female orgasm usually consists of 3 to 10 muscular contractions less than a second apart.

Refractory ♂ period

This is a rest period that males experience right after ejaculation. For the vast majority of men, no matter how hard they try to get an erection during this time, it won't work. The refractory period can last 10 minutes or much longer. The older you are, the longer you'll have to wait to get your erection back.

The benefits of orgasm

- It feels really good and sometimes unbelievably fantastic.
- The release of tension helps some people sleep at night.
- It can leave you feeling very close and at ease with your partner.
- It can relieve period pains.

Ovaries

These are the female gonads. There are 2 of them, each about the size of an almond. When a female child is born, her ovaries hold up to 400,000 female sex cells between them. Once a month for as long as a woman menstruates, one of those cells, in either the left or right ovary, matures into an egg. The ovary then releases the egg into the nearest fallopian tube.

Ovulation ♀

This is when a mature egg is released from one of the ovaries and drawn into the nearest fallopian tube. For the next 2 days the egg travels down the tube, taking its time just in case any sperm show up (conception usually takes place in the fallopian tubes). Most women don't feel anything when they ovulate, though it's possible to notice a slight twinge or cramp in the abdomen. What's more common is to see a change in your vaginal discharge. Around ovulation it becomes clear and slippery, and there's more of it. The reason behind this is simple: secretions in the vagina change to create a more welcoming environment for sperm. This is the time in your cycle when it's easiest to get pregnant. Women ovulate monthly until menopause.

Once in a while, the ovary releases 2 eggs. If both are fertilized and both embryos successfully implant on the uterine wall, the result will be non-identical twins. If one fertilized egg divides into 2, identical twins will develop.

Parents

You may have one parent or 2, or even 3 or 4. These are the adults who are raising you to make your way in the world. Whether or not they're doing a great job of preparing you for life, your parents probably love you and want to keep you from harm. This includes helping you cope with the risks and difficulties of being sexually active. While you may not feel like talking about sex with your parents, if you have a real problem, they'll probably know something about where you're coming from. And there's a good chance they'll want to help.

Peer Pressure

Building on long-standing stereotypes, the people who manufacture pop culture use video, television, movies, and advertising to pump out the message that image is every-thing. Not just any image, but one that's defined by thin, sculpted bodies, beautiful faces, amazing hair, highly stylized clothing, smart accessories, and, to tie it all together, sex. According to pop culture, if you manage your image well, you'll be sexy, desirable, and valuable. The pressure to conform is unrelenting. Many teenagers keep up the pressure by judging each other based on the standards set by "the image."

In females

Girls are expected to be sexually available. This isn't the same as being interested in sex or expressive about their feelings of desire. It's about being alluring and receptive to sexual advances. Girls who refuse to have sex can be dismissed for their immaturity or worthlessness. Or they can be disliked for their stubbornness. Wanting to avoid dismissal and shame, or wanting to please, many girls decide to have sex, even though their reasons for not wanting to are excellent ones (see opposite page). Ironically, girls who are sexually active or who deliberately try to be alluring (for example, by wearing provocative clothing) can be labelled sluts.

In males

Guys are expected to be accomplished studs who want sex all the time. Very little emphasis is placed on building a loving, trusting relationship that culminates in sex.

Guys who refuse to be aggressive about sex can have their masculinity ridiculed, mostly by their male peers. They can be taunted for being weaklings or accused of being homosexual. Given our homophobic society and the fact that homophobia is rampant at most secondary schools, being labelled homosexual can be very frightening. Hoping to avoid the contempt of their peers and even physical abuse, many guys decide to have sex, even though their reasons for not wanting to are excellent ones (see opposite).

Saying no

Everyone has the right to say no, even at the last minute, even if you love the person you're with. Saying no can be hard or even traumatic, but if you're uncomfortable with the situation, the sex will probably be bad, either physically, emotionally, or both. Yuck. Avoiding lousy sex has other advantages—you won't have to worry about pregnancy and sexually transmitted infections. Saying no is easier if you've decided in advance exactly how far you want to go. It's even easier if you know what your reasons are and feel solid about them.

Reasons to not want to have sex

- I don't feel turned on
- The setting isn't right
- No one has protection
- It goes against my morals
- I don't like the person enough
- I don't feel well
- There's too much pressure
- I don't trust the person
- I don't know what I'm doing
- Someone might walk in
- I'm not in love
- The relationship isn't what I want it to be
- I want to wait
- I've got other things on my mind

Penis ♂

- dick
- cock
- rod
- tackle
- nob
- pecker
- prick
- schlong
- John Thomas
- willy
- wanger

Biology

The penis is made up of 2 parts: a head, also called a glans, and a shaft. The head is extremely sensitive due to the many nerve endings that are distributed over its surface (smaller penises tend to orgasm earlier due to having the same number of nerve endings concentrated over a smaller surface). The shaft is far less sensitive. When the penis is flaccid (soft), the skin that covers the shaft is loose and wrinkly. During an erection, the skin becomes taut. In an uncircumcised penis, the skin of the shaft extends up and over the head, creating a protective hood. This is the foreskin. A circumcised penis has no foreskin. (Circumsion means having the foreskin removed, usually just after birth. Research suggests that the penis head is no less sensitive as a result of losing its protective hood.)

When it comes to penises, what everyone seems to want to know about is size: how big does it have to be to satisfy a lover? To satisfy the male ego? What does a girl need to see to sit up and take notice? Or a guy? Can a penis ever be too big? How small is too small?

With all this talk of penis size, the burning question is, how does an average penis measure up? It's interesting to note that every sex book answers this question with different figures, which is proof that penis size (and width) varies from guy to guy, and that there's no "correct" size. Taking the lowest and highest figures that are out there, the average penis, when soft, is between 6 and 12 cm long. The average penis, when hard, measures between 10 and 20 cm.

At first glance, penis size appears to be important. In terms of sex, very big penises can be alarming to some people, and very small ones can seem inadequate. In terms of ego, the macho stereotype tells us that the bigger the penis, the more masculine—sexy, strong, powerful—the guy. Also, because males are very visual, they're more likely to be impressed or turned on by what they see, and big penises (like big breasts) are visually stimulating.

The truth is, penis size doesn't really matter. Where sex is concerned, satisfying your partner has far more to do with how imaginative, sensitive, and

Penis

knowledgeable about sex you are than with the proportions of your penis. A wee weenie or an extra long schlong is rarely the cause of poor sex. In intercourse, since most of the vagina's nerve endings are around the opening and just inside, even a short penis can stimulate vaginal pleasure. In terms of ego, more and more people are clued in to the fact that masculinity has nothing to do with penis size. As for males being more visual than females, that's true, but when it comes to falling in love or getting blown away by sexual chemistry, it's the whole person that makes it happen, not the appendages.

Too big, too small?

For vaginal sex

Very large, long penises can make some girls nervous. They're afraid of being hurt during intercourse, and with good reason. If a girl isn't sufficiently lubricated—and fear can stop lubrication in the bat of an eye—putting your penis in will be painful. Deep, hard thrusting will also be painful as your penis whacks up against her cervix. But none of this means your penis is too big. What it means is that you have to know a couple of things and approach your partner with sensitivity, which is always a turn-on anyway. Here are the things you need to know:

1. All vaginas are very elastic. If they can stretch enough to allow a baby to go through, they can stretch to fit your penis. The trick is to make her vagina physically ready. This can be achieved through excellent foreplay (long and sweet) and, if necessary, plenty of shop-bought lubrication.

2. Don't plan on deep penetration, at least not the first time you make love. Also, certain positions give her more control, like when she's on top or the 2 of you are on your side. If she needs to move away a bit, she can. Knowing this, she'll be

Inside the penis is the urethra, which is the passageway for urine and semen. There are also 3 columns of spongy tissue that become engorged with blood during sexual stimulation. The blood rushes to the penis, then is trapped there when the blood vessels leading away from the penis constrict. What you get when this happens is an erection.

The size of a guy's hands, feet, and nose tells you absolutely nothing about the size of his penis.

Generally, a guy's penis will have reached its adult proportion by the time he turns 18.

more relaxed. Take it slowly. As you get used to each other, chances are you'll be able to penetrate more deeply over time.

If your penis is very small and you can't penetrate deeply, why not make the most of all the other ways you can be an incredible lover? It's a wide open field, and most girls will appreciate that you're willing to play it. After all, penetration alone rarely results in orgasm for the majority of women. Find out where your partner likes to be kissed and touched. Experiment with oral sex and anal stimulation. Play with genital masturbation, including masturbating her with your penis. Become expert at sensual massage. When it comes to penetration, there are a few things to know:

1. Make love in positions that change the slant of her vagina, leaving it less open. For example, she could be on top, but leaning back, or you could try entering her from behind. Positions that increase friction are also good, such as missionary style but with her legs close together rather than spread wide open.

2. You probably don't have to worry about hurting her with hard, deep thrusting, so go for it (with her permission, of course).

MEATUS (opening to urethra)
HEAD
FRENULUM
SHAFT
TESTES
SCROTUM

For anal sex

When it comes to anal sex, some people have no fear of large penises, while others find them intimidating. The anus isn't elastic like the vagina, so there's not much chance of stretching. Even masses of lubrication won't be helpful. For those who find large penises daunting, there are many other ways to discover sexual pleasure with a partner. Or they may have a partner with a narrow penis that's shorter in length. Such a penis could provide a comfortable fit. Not only would the head be a closer match for the anus, but the length would provide excellent stimulation given the fact that deep penetration is neither advised nor liked by many people.
See Anal Sex.

Period Pains ♀

⟍cramps ⟍dysmenorrhoea

Before or during a girl's period, and even during
ovulation, she may feel pain in her abdomen. It can
be so mild she hardly notices it or so sharp she has
to lie down. According to recent research, what's
behind this pain is an overproduction of prostaglandins.
These substances set in motion a clenching and
relaxing of the uterine muscles, called contractions,
that help push the menstrual flow out the uterus.
When too many prostaglandins are produced, usually
at the beginning of menstruation, the contractions
are very severe and they hurt. In many women,
severe contractions reduce the blood
supply to the area, causing lower backache.

Prostaglandins that enter the bloodstream are
also responsible for the nausea and diarrhoea experienced
by some girls during their period. Severe pain during
menstruation that lasts for more than 3 days should
be checked out by a doctor. See Cystitis, Endometriosis,
IUD, and Pelvic Inflammatory Disease for other causes
of abdominal cramping.

Treatment

Once menstrual cramps set in, there are many things you can
do to ease the pain. Gentle exercise works for lots of women.
According to some reports, so does orgasm. Many women
practise relaxation techniques, acupuncture, and yoga. Others
are comforted by drinking herbal teas or adding vitamin and
mineral supplements to their diet. For some women, the best
remedies include putting a hot-water bottle or heating pad on
their abdomen or back, taking a warm bath, or lying in a knee-
to-chest position. If you're interested in trying medication, ask
your doctor about nonsteroidal anti-inflammatories, which act
against prostaglandins.

Prevention

Adopting a healthy lifestyle will go a long way to diminishing cramps, though it may not eliminate them completely. For starters, eat a good balance of nutritious foods. Next, find out if you have any food allergies. Eating foods you're allergic to can produce an excess of the prostaglandins that cause cramping. On the other hand, eating fish rich in Omega-3 fatty acids (salmon, tuna, whitefish, and sardines) may help suppress the production of prostaglandins. Avoiding over-processed foods can make a big difference to the way you feel, as can limiting your intake of salt, sugar, alcohol, and caffeine.

It's also important to get enough sleep, to exercise regularly, and to keep stress to a minimum. In our fast-paced, junk-food culture, this is asking a lot! But do what you can. A naturopathic doctor can help you explore diet and the effects it has on the body.

If further prevention is needed, ask your doctor about the birth control pill, which stops the production of prostaglandins. Your doctor can also give you advice about prescription medications that inhibit cramping. Or try taking an over-the-counter painkiller such as ibuprofen, which blocks the production of prostaglandins. Ibuprofen can be taken up to 2 days before your period starts, or at the very latest, at the first hint of cramps. Taken later, once the cramping is in full swing, it may have less effect. **See Menstruation, PMS.**

Menstrual cramps are not imaginary. Symptoms such as abdominal pain, lower backache, sweating, chills, dizziness, feeling faint, diarrhoea, nausea, fatigue, and irritability are real. Some girls have them and others don't.

pelvic inflammatory disease

↘

An infection of the cervix becomes PID once it spreads to the uterus and fallopian tubes. When this happens, the fallopian tubes can become blocked by scarring. Complete blockage results in infertility, even in teenagers. Partial blockage can lead to an ectopic pregnancy, which is life-threatening. Wearing an IUD can make it easier for an infection to spread into the cervix and through the uterus.

The most common causes of PID are chlamydia and gonorrhoea, which start out as simple infections that can easily be cured by taking antibiotics. A cure at this stage means that no permanent damage will be done to your reproductive system. Unfortunately, millions of women don't get treated for chlamydia and gonorrhoea because they don't have any symptoms and don't realize they're infected. As a result, the infection spreads and becomes PID.

You can suspect you have PID if you have pain in your pelvic area or if it suddenly hurts to have intercourse. Other symptoms include fever, vomiting, headaches, unpleasant discharge, and unusual periods (painful, very heavy flow, spotting between periods) All of these symptoms can be mild or intense, and some people have no symptoms at all. See Chlamydia, Douching, Ectopic Pregnancy, Gonorrhoea, IUD.

Getting tested

If you're sexually active the easiest way to avoid PID is to use a condom every time you have intercourse. If you've had sex without a condom, you should get tested for chlamydia and gonorrhoea about 2 weeks afterwards. A negative test may not be accurate, so if you think your partner was infected, get tested again. Don't wait for symptoms, because often there aren't any. If you're in a long-term relationship, you should get tested for these infections once a year (to protect yourself in case your partner has strayed).

Treatment

PID can be cured by taking antibiotics, but that doesn't mean there won't be damage to your fallopian tubes. To minimize the damage, rest in bed and avoid intercourse until the infection is gone. In some cases, severe damage requires surgery. The more often you have PID, the greater your chances of becoming infertile and the greater your risk of having an ectopic pregnancy.

Prevention

The best prevention against PID is to practise safer sex and to get tested regularly. Using an IUD as birth control isn't recommended. Avoid douching.

PMS ♀

↘premenstrual syndrome

The female body produces oestrogen and progesterone, which are hormones that regulate the menstrual cycle. While regulating the cycle, these hormones influence the body in other ways, some of which may be negative. For example, month after month, many girls experience a variety of unpleasant symptoms in the days leading up to their period. The symptoms may be emotional (depression, tearfulness, confusion, anxiety, irritability) or physical (bloating, headaches, fatigue, insomnia, food cravings, tenderness in the breasts, clumsiness) or both. Put together, these symptoms have been labelled premenstrual syndrome, known to most people as PMS.

Many women never experience PMS, or it only starts later in life. For those who have PMS beginning in adolescence, symptoms are usually mild, but in some girls they're so intense that they inter-fere with daily life. The symptoms show up between 2 and 12 days before the start of each period and usually stop less than a day later. Girls with severe PMS look for ways to soften their symptoms. Some report that yoga is helpful, or taking evening primrose oil or small doses of vitamin B6. For the majority of women, the best way to keep PMS to a minimum is to maintain a healthy diet and a regular exercise programme. It also helps to have the understanding of friends and family. If you have PMS that's completely disruptive, see a doctor or naturopath who has experience in this area. See Period Pains.

Pre-ejaculate ♂

↘pre-come ↘pre-cun

When a guy's penis is erect and excited, a clear or milky fluid called pre-ejaculate sometimes appears at the tip. This fluid isn't semen, but it can contain sperm, which means a girl can get pregnant if it comes into contact with her vagina. If you're a guy, you should know that because of pre-come, taking your penis out of your girlfriend's vagina just before ejaculating is not a form of birth control. Pre-ejaculate can also contain viruses and bacteria. See Withdrawal.

Q & A ♀

Q: My boyfriend was really excited when we were in a hot tub together. Could I be pregnant if his pre-ejaculate got into the water?

A: No. It's not possible for you to get pregnant by sperm that's released in water. To get pregnant, his penis would have to make direct contact with your vagina.

Q: Can I get pregnant from anal sex?

A: No. The only way you can get pregnant is if semen or pre-ejaculate come into contact with your vagina. But you still need protection from sexually transmitted infections that can be transmitted during anal sex. Make sure your boyfriend wears a condom.

Q: I had sex with my boyfriend, then a few days later I got my period. Is it possible I'm pregnant?

A: If your period was on time and you don't have any symptoms of pregnancy, such as needing to pee a lot or vomiting in the morning, you're probably not pregnant. In rare cases, a girl could be pregnant and have vaginal bleeding that looks like menstrual flow.

Pregnancy ♀

A woman is considered to be pregnant when a fertilized egg implants on the wall of her uterus. There are 3 ways this can happen: if a guy thrusts his penis inside her vagina and ejaculates; if a guy slips his penis quickly into her vagina and pulls out before he comes, but pre-ejaculate from the tip of his penis leaves sperm in the vagina; if a guy makes a decision not to penetrate, but ejaculates near the entrance to her vagina. In each scenario, sperm has a good chance of making it to an egg and fertilizing it.

If you think you're pregnant (you missed your period, your breasts are tender, you feel bloated, you throw up every morning, you're unusually tired, you need to pee a lot) find out for sure by going to a chemists and buying a home pregnancy test. If the test is positive, you're pregnant—an embryo is growing in your uterus. Over the next 9 months the embryo will grow into a foetus that will continue to develop until it's a baby ready to be born. Do you want the baby? If you do, how will your life change? If you're not ready to be a mother and you don't want the baby, what are you going to do? There's a lot to think about.

If you're pregnant you have 3 choices: keep the baby, give the baby up for adoption, or have an abortion. This is a big, serious decision. Try to talk about it with someone trustworthy who loves you, such as your parents, an aunt, a friend, or your boyfriend. It's usually helpful to get the advice of a professional who is trained to help teens in your situation, such as a nurse at a clinic or a school counsellor. Another option is to call a telephone hotline for information. If you're considering abortion, the decision must be made quickly. **See Abortion, Emergency Contraception.**

Pregnancy will happen within the year if you're having unprotected sex on a regular basis. Even if you use protection, pregnancy is a possibility because no birth control method is 100% effective.

Protection

If you're sexually active there are a couple of things you can do to lower your risk of catching sexually transmitted infections. There are also a variety of things you can use that will help you avoid pregnancy. All these "things" are actually important methods of protection. Some work better than others. To be effective, they all must be used correctly. When checking out the types of protection available, remember that not all of them protect against STIs. Carefully read about each one before making your choice.

It's much easier to use protection when you're being sexual with someone you trust and are comfortable talking to. There's also a better chance you'll use it if you and your partner decide ahead of time what kind of protection is right for you as a couple. In situations where the sex is spontaneous, your determination to use protection might not weaken if you practise ahead of time what you'll say if your partner resists using it.

Protection that lowers the risk of pregnancy

- ⬊ Implanon
- ⬊ The Pill
- ⬊ Depo-Provera
- ⬊ Condom
- ⬊ Condom with spermicide
- ⬊ Female condom with spermicide
- ⬊ Diaphragm with spermicide
- ⬊ Cervical cap with spermicide
- ⬊ Sponge

Protection that lowers the risk of contracting some STIs

- ⬊ Condom
- ⬊ Condom with spermicide
- ⬊ Female condom with spermicide
- ⬊ Diaphragm with spermicide
- ⬊ Spermicide on its own
- ⬊ Dam

In males

The signs of puberty show up shortly after your testicles begin producing large amounts of testosterone. This usually happens between the ages of 12 and 16. Changes include bigger testicles and a bigger penis, the growth of pubic hair, body hair and facial hair, oilier skin, sweating, a deeper voice, and the development of stronger muscles. Lots of guys get tall suddenly. For guys, the biggest event in puberty is the first time they ejaculate. When this happens unexpectedly one night when they're asleep, it can be confusing and embarrassing. When it happens in the waking hours as a result of masturbation, it can be a triumph.

Puberty

This is the incredible period of growth during the last few years of your childhood when your body goes through many changes. You also begin to think about sex and have sexual feelings. Puberty lasts 2 to 3 years, and on the day you're capable of reproduction, it's over. It can be an emotionally intense time because of everything that's happening in your body.

In females ♀

Puberty begins when the ovaries start producing oestrogen in large amounts, which usually happens between the ages of 8 and 14. The oestrogen triggers other events, such as breast and hip development, the arrival of hair on various body parts (vulva, armpits, upper lip, toes), and a growth spurt, where body fat increases from 8% to 21 or 22%. Your skin becomes oilier, you discover what it feels like to sweat, and from time to time you notice a white, sticky discharge on your underwear. For most girls, the biggest event in puberty is when their first period starts. Some girls are really excited and proud when this happens, others are sad to leave their childhood behind, and still others have mixed emotions, including apprehension about what this new reality will bring.

Pubic Lice

↘crabs

People who have a persistent itch in their crotch often discover they have pubic lice. At first they can't believe it—no one wants to think that insects are living on their skin—but in fact pubic lice are common. They thrive anywhere on the human body that's moist and hairy, including armpits, beards, and eyelashes. Occasionally they make their home in chest hair, around the anus, and on the scalp. But crabs are mostly found in the crotch, probably because they're usually passed from one person to the next through genital contact. They're very contagious. Because crabs can survive for 24 hours without food (human blood), they can also be picked up from infested clothing, towels, bed sheets, blankets, furniture, toilet seats, and even the family pet. Through scratching, crabs can be transferred from one location on the body to another, as long as the second location has hair.

Pubic lice are yellowish-grey in colour. They earned the nickname "crabs" because they look so much like the crabs that are found at the seashore. They live for about a month, eating blood and laying eggs every day. Each egg is attached to a single hair and takes about a week to hatch. Even an egg that's fallen with a hair onto the floor or a pillow will hatch a week after it was laid. The eggs, also known as nits, can be seen under a magnifying glass. Adult crabs can be seen with the naked eye. The itching people feel is actually the crabs biting into their skin. Some people with crabs hardly feel any itching at all and don't realize they have them.

Getting Tested

Adult crabs are about the size of a pinhead and are easily identified by people who know what they look like. For a self-diagnosis, use a magnifying glass. If what you see moves, it's probably crabs. For confirmation, go to a health clinic where a nurse or doctor will tell you exactly what you have and how to treat it.

Prevention

Don't have physical contact with someone who complains of an unexplained itch. Think twice before borrowing someone's clothing or sleeping in a strange bed.

Treatment

Soaps that contain pesticides are available over the counter and by prescription. These are very effective at killing crabs if you follow the instructions carefully. Pesticides can harm your eyes, so if you have crabs in your eyelashes, ask your doctor for an alternative treatment. When the treatment is done, remove all nits either by tweezing the hair or cutting it off close to the skin. To make sure there are no nits anywhere waiting to hatch, wash all your sheets and blankets in very hot water, then dry in a hot dryer. Or send them to the dry cleaners. Do the same to the clothes you wore while you were infected. Keep watching for crabs and nits for a couple of weeks, just in case one survived. To stop the spread of these bugs, tell your partner, or other partners in the previous month, that you had them.

Queer

For decades, many people used the word "queer" in a derogatory way to describe homosexuals and homosexual activity. Nowadays, queer is used very differently. It proudly describes individuals, behaviours, and ideas that don't fit neatly into standard sex and gender categories. People who consider themselves queer may include lesbians, gay men, bisexuals, transsexuals, transvestites, and anyone else who expresses their sexuality in unique ways. One of the attractions of the word is that there's no single set of characteristics that limits what queer is. At best, it can be defined as any sexual response or expression that doesn't conform to society's gender expectations. Since the early 1990s, a growing number of urban centres have set up queer networks that offer support, advice, and community to anyone struggling with issues surrounding queer sexuality. (Go to www.queeryouth.org.uk for more info.)

Between 70 and 80% of all rapes are date rapes. They usually happen during the last year of school and the first year of sixth-form college.

When someone says no to sex, it means they don't want it. No means no every time. Don't even play with the idea that no means yes. It doesn't.

Rape
↘sexual assault

When a guy forces a girl to have intercourse against her will, it's rape. It doesn't matter how short her skirt was or how she was behaving or how many guys she'd had sex with in the past or whether or not she knew her attacker; forced sex is rape, and it's a crime. The force can be exerted verbally, through threats or intimidation, or physically, through violence. It's also rape when a girl forces another girl to have sex, when a girl uses psychological manipulation to make a guy have sex with her, and when a guy forces another guy to have anal sex.

Even though rape is a form of sexual assault, it isn't really about sex. It's usually about a guy using his penis in a violent way to exert power over another human being. The rapist feels boosted and powerful and walks away with his ego soaring. This can be the case even if the rapist is a boyfriend or husband. How the victim feels is unique to that individual, but common reactions include terror, self-blame, incredible anger, depression, and extreme feelings of helplessness and distrust. Girls who force guys to have sex with them are on a similar power trip.

Date Rape
↘acquaintance rape

Date rape is usually when a girl is raped by a guy she knows. It could be her boyfriend, her brother's friend, a co-worker, someone she's on a date with, or a guy she talked to for a while at a party. Often there's an initial attraction between the girl and the guy. Eventually they start to fool around. At one point the girl wants to stop, but the guy won't let her and ends up raping her. Some guys don't even realize they've done anything wrong. It's also date rape when the girl is so drunk or stoned that she can't say no to sex and is penetrated while she's really out of it or after passing out. In rare cases, it's the girl who forces the guy to have intercourse. When he wants to stop, she threatens his masculinity by accusing him of being a coward or a weakling, or by suggesting that he's homosexual.

Date Rape Drugs

- ↘ roofies
- ↘ rohypnol
- ↘ GHB

There are 2 drugs that are used to sedate victims so they can easily be raped. One is a pill called rohypnol, or "roofie" for short. The other is gamma hydroxybutirate (GHB), which is a clear, slightly salty liquid. Both drugs are tranquilizers. GHB can put you into a deep sleep, while a roofie can make you feel paralyzed, dizzy, or spaced out. It can also cause victims to forget everything that happened while they were drugged. Date rape drugs are usually slipped into a drink, which is then offered to the victim. They can also be put into food. To avoid the possibility of being drugged, then raped, don't accept drinks or food from people you don't know and trust, don't share your drinks, and never let your glass or bottle out of your sight.
See Sexual Assault.

No one secretly enjoys being raped. Rape is always ugly and usually terrifying.

Finding help after being raped

There are many people who are specially trained to help rape victims by offering comfort, advice, and practical information. See Resources at the end of the book.

Ready for Sex

If you feel ready for sex and your partner feels ready too, there's no reason why you shouldn't have a good experience together. Being ready means:

- ✓ feeling comfortable with your body and with your feelings of desire
- ✓ feeling comfortable with sex on a moral level
- ✓ being knowledgeable about your body
- ✓ caring about the well-being of your partner
- ✓ being able to talk openly with your partner about what you like and don't like
- ✓ knowing you can say "no" at any time, even at the last minute
- ✓ having an agreement with your partner about which protection you'll use to avoid sexually transmitted infections and pregnancy, then using the protection properly
- ✓ knowing what your options are if you get pregnant, or, if you're a guy, your girlfriend gets pregnant
- ✓ knowing what to do if you become infected with a sexually transmitted infection

See Bad Sex, Communication, First Sex.

Respect

Before respect, there's esteem. Esteem means holding someone or something in high regard. For example, people with good self-esteem think well of themselves and believe they're worth something. As a result, they don't let themselves get into too many negative situations, where people mistreat them or where the risk of danger is high—or if they find themselves in negative situations, they get out of there fast. People with good self-esteem take care of themselves. They treat themselves with respect. To do this consistently, they need to be good listeners, particularly to their own hearts. People who listen to their hearts find it easier to make decisions that are right for them. In some cases decisions happen instinctively (knowing what's right comes in a flash), in others, it takes time to think things through.

Respect is also something that people give to others. In general, individuals who are in the habit of treating themselves with care and respect don't find it too hard to extend the same behaviour to friends and strangers. To do this well, they need to be skilled at listening so they can hear the needs and desires expressed by others. Respecting others is always good, but only when it goes hand in hand with respecting yourself. For example, if you're in a relationship with someone who disrespects you by treating you badly, your priority is to show respect for yourself by leaving the relationship.

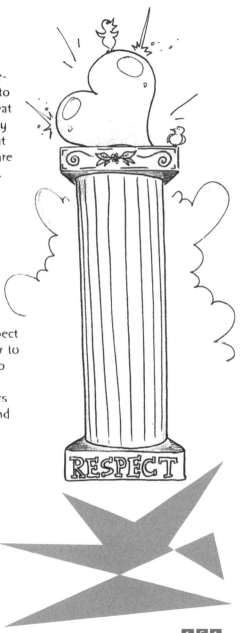

Having respect for yourself and your partner will help you make the right choices about sex.

Rhythm Method
↘calendar method

As birth control, the rhythm method is unreliable. The object is to have intercourse when the woman isn't in the fertile part of her cycle—when there's no egg awaiting fertilization in one of the fallopian tubes. This way, according to the plan, she won't get pregnant. But to determine when she isn't fertile, it's necessary to know when she is.

Peak fertility occurs at the time of ovulation, which usually happens mid-cycle. If the woman's cycle is regular, she can look at her calendar and determine when mid-cycle will be. The trouble is, cycles are frequently irregular, especially in teenagers, so her prediction may be off. Finally, because the egg travels through the fallopian tube for a couple days, and sperm can live in the female reproductive system for several days, it's impossible to know when the "safe days" are. Of couples using the rhythm method, 20% become pregnant in the first year.
See Birth Control, Menstrual Cycle, Ovulation.

Rimming
↘analingus
↘ring dhobi

Stimulating your partner's anus with your tongue is called rimming.

Rimming
Protection

Rimming brings saliva into contact with the anus, but so far there have been no reported cases of getting infected with HIV this way. If your partner has syphilis, however, you can easily become infected if you touch open sores on his or her anus, or you can infect your partner if you have open sores on your mouth. Herpes is also easily traded during rimming, whether or not sores are present. Also, it's possible to ingest faecal matter while rimming, which means you can catch intestinal parasites if your partner has them, as well as hepatitis A if the faecal matter is infected.

It's not the sexiest of solutions, but if you're uncomfortable with the thought that your partner may have an infection, you can place a dam over the anus before rimming. Putting a bit of lubricant under the dam will increase the pleasure for your partner. Using a dam will also protect you from bacteria that may be lingering in the area. See Anal Sex, Anus.

Safe Sex

For a long time people used the term "safe sex" to refer to sex with a condom—and then they realized that condoms weren't 100% effective and that the accurate term for sex with a condom, or with any kind of protection, was actually "safer sex." Once in a while you still hear people referring to safe sex, but sex that's truly safe only includes a few activities, such as holding hands, hugging, breast and chest fondling, and pressing your fully clothed body up against the fully clothed body of the person you're hot for. Any other kind of sex can lead to one or more infections, even if you're protected. For example, condoms offer excellent protection against some infections, but less protection against herpes, genital warts, syphilis, crabs, and molluscum contagiosum. If a condom isn't used correctly, breaks during use, or is defective, transmission of HIV and other STIs is possible. When it comes to pregnancy, there are several very effective birth control methods on the market, but none works 100% of the time, even when used correctly every time.

Safer Sex

Enjoying sexual activities without thinking about the consequences exists only on TV and in fantasyland. Without-a-care-in-the-world sex simply isn't an option for people who aren't in long-term monogamous relationships, no matter how easy it is to pretend otherwise. Even long-term couples still have to think about pregnancy. No sexual act is guaranteed safe, which leaves you with 2 choices: abstinence or safer sex. Safer sex may not sound very exciting at first, but if you consider the alternatives, it will start to grow on you. Unintended pregnancies and STIs are no picnic.

Safer sex means taking action to minimize the exchange of body fluids—blood, semen, vaginal fluids—between you and your partner. These fluids can contain viruses and bacteria, and to remain safe, you must avoid coming into contact with them. Using a condom—for intercourse, anal sex, and oral sex on a guy—or using a dam—for oral sex on a woman—are the best ways you can achieve this.

Safer sex also means avoiding 4 kinds of skin-to-skin contact—genital-to-genital, mouth-to-genital, mouth-to-anus, and genital to anus. This is necessary because viruses and bacteria can be present in sores or bumps on the skin. Unfortunately, herpes and several other STIs can be present on skin that can't be covered by a condom. Dams, which come in 15cm squares, and female condoms cut open (or latex gloves cut open), will cover more area. To find out how to wring a bit of fun out of these useful latex products, see Condoms and Dams.

Another thing you can do to minimize your chances of catching sexually transmitted infections is to limit the number of partners you have. Because having sex with one person exposes you to all of his or her previous sexual contacts, your exposure is significantly decreased with every partner you turn down.

Last but not least, practising safer sex means making testing a routine part of your health care. If you engage in sexual activities with numerous partners, it's important to get tested a couple of times a year, or every time you have a new partner. Because several STIs have few or no symptoms, testing is the only way you can tell that you have them. If you treat gonorrhoea, chlamydia, and syphilis early, you won't be left with long-term damage.

Q & A

Q: Is it safe to have unprotected intercourse when my girlfriend has her period?

A: Even though she has her period, it's possible for her to get pregnant. It's also possible for either of you to catch a sexually transmitted infection if one of you is already infected. If she has HIV, her menstrual flow carries a significant amount of the virus, more than her usual vaginal secretions.

Safer sex activities include kissing, caressing, massage, sharing erotic fantasies, and mutual masturbation.

Q & A ♀

Q: Is it better to wear pads or tampons during menstruation?

A: This is a matter of personal comfort. Some girls prefer pads, others swear by tampons, and many use both. Some women use a new product called a Keeper.

Tips

⬎ Menstrual fluid is odourless until it leaves the body. Not long after it contacts the air it begins to smell slightly. The smell becomes stronger the longer the blood is exposed. To avoid an unpleasant odour, remove your pad when it's nearly soaked and put on a new one. On light days, change your pad every 4 hours or so.

⬎ Perfumed pads can irritate the skin. Use unscented ones.

⬎ Pads clog toilets, so wrap your used pads in toilet paper and put them in the bin.

⬎ Non-chlorine-bleached pads can be purchased in health food shops or on-line.

Sanitary Towels
⬎pads ⬎pantyliners

Over the centuries women have placed all kinds of materials next to their vaginal openings to soak up their menstrual flow, including natural sponges, wool, papyrus, grass, paper, and cloth. The modern equivalent of these old-time methods is pads. Made from soft cotton and plastic, pads come in a variety of shapes, lengths, and thicknesses. An adhesive strip runs along the bottom of each pad to hold it firmly in place against the wearer's undies.

When girls first start menstruating, they usually use pads. Sooner or later, most of them switch to tampons, though more likely to a combination of pads and tampons. For example, many girls use tampons during the day and when their flow is medium to heavy, and pads at night and on days when their flow is light. It's also common to use pads as backup for tampons on very heavy days. Some girls are only comfortable using pads.

Improvements in technology have made today's pads thin, absorbent, invisible through clothing, and comfortable. However, not everyone advocates using the commercial variety. Some women would prefer to see their peers purchasing reusable cloth pads or making their own (special cloth and instructions can be ordered on the Internet). This would be a step toward solving the world's landfill problem. Cloth pads may even be safer if it's proven that chlorine-bleached cotton delivers toxins through the vagina and into the body. A relatively new product that catches menstrual flow is called the Keeper. According to reports, it's safe, environmentally friendly, and convenient.
See Keeper, Tampons.

Scabies

These microscopic bugs annoy their human hosts by their constant activity. The females burrow under the skin to lay their eggs. As they burrow, they produce secretions that will eventually cause an allergic reaction in their host. When the females have laid all their eggs, they die. Several days later the eggs hatch and the larvae travel to the surface, where they forage in the skin for food as they grow into adults. The females mate and, like their predecessors, burrow under the skin to lay their eggs. More secretions are produced. Four weeks after infection with scabies, the allergic reaction to the first secretions shows up as small, red sores or blisters, often in line formation. These sores can be severely itchy, especially at night.

Scabies (pronounced SCAY-bees) can infest any area of the body, though they prefer locations where the skin is warm, moist, and folded—around ankles, wrists, breasts, fingers, feet, buttocks, the vulva, and the penis. Highly contagious, they're passed from one person to another by skin-to-skin contact. The contact can be sexual or casual. Scabies can also be picked up from infested clothing, towels, bed sheets, and blankets, where they can survive for up to 48 hours.

Getting tested

Early detection is important, so if you have even the smallest suspicion that these parasites have taken up residence in your skin, see a doctor. He or she will take a small scraping from one of your sores and examine it under a microscope. Many people mistake scabies for other skin conditions such as eczema.

Treatment

Your doctor will prescribe a medicated cream or recommend one you can buy over the counter. Treatment usually involves spreading the cream over your entire body before bed, then washing it off in the morning. Some people repeat this treatment to make sure that every last egg is dead. It's also necessary to wash sheets and blankets in very hot water, then dry them in a hot dryer. Sending them out to be dry-cleaned will also remove the scabies. Recently worn clothing should also be carefully washed and dried. It may take up to 4 weeks for the sores to heal. As soon as possible, tell your partner, or other recent partners, that you had scabies. There's a good chance they have them too.

Prevention

If a prospective partner is itching a lot, there's a reason for it. Check for small red sores or blisters that look like they may be hiding burrowing insects. If you're even slightly suspicious, put off sexual contact with that person until a doctor has diagnosed the cause of the itch, prescribed a treatment, and the treatment has been successfully completed.

Q: Is lumpy semen a cause for concern?

A: Not everyone's semen is the same. Yours may be yellowish in colour or white or even transparent. If it's a bit lumpy, that's okay. Some guys make stringy semen, others make it smooth. Odour and taste can also change from guy to guy.

Q: What if a guy ejaculates, touches his semen with his fingers, then puts his fingers in my vagina. Can I get pregnant?

A: Sperm have to be wet to stay alive, so if the semen dries or gets rubbed off before his fingers go in, you won't get pregnant. But if the semen is fresh and wet, it's as if he's delivering the sperm right to the door, and yes, you could get pregnant.

Scrotum

This is the sac of hairy skin that hangs below the penis and holds the testicles. Very sensitive to touch, many men enjoy having it fondled during sex. The scrotum has the important job of keeping the testicles at just the right temperature to make sperm.

Semen

↘come ↘jism ↘wad
↘cum ↘spunk ↘load

This is the sticky fluid that shoots out of the penis, usually during orgasm. Each ejaculation of semen contains fluids from various glands and about 400 million sperm. Semen can carry the HIV virus, hepatitis B, the germs that cause chlamydia and gonorrhoea, and the trich parasite, which causes trichomoniasis.

Sex

When people talk about someone's sex, they're referring to that person's female or male biology. This is determined at conception when a sperm fertilizes an egg. The result is a single cell called a zygote. Inside the zygote are 23 pairs of chromosomes. The first 22 pairs are matched. The last pair, called the sex chromosomes, can be similar (**XX**) or different (**XY**). A zygote with **XX** chromosomes will develop into a female child with female sex characteristics (vulva, breasts). A zygote with **XY** chromosomes will develop into a male child with male sex characteristics (penis, testicles). Sex is not the same as gender. See Gender, Hermaphrodite.

Sexual Abuse

Touching, fondling, kissing, oral sex, intercourse, and any other sexual behaviour that one person forces on another is sexual abuse. Often the abuser is someone in a position of trust and authority, such as a teacher, babysitter, priest, coach, or family friend. As such, he or she is able to persuade the victim, through gentle insistence, frightening threats, or physical violence, to behave as demanded. When sexual abuse happens inside a family—perpetrated by the father, brother, grandfather, or uncle—it's called incest. Rarely, cases have been reported of mothers abusing their sons or daughters and of women in positions of authority abusing boys or girls. Abuse frequently continues over several years.

It's common for children and teenagers in this situation, despite their innocence and terror and unhappiness, to blame themselves for their abuser's behaviour. They feel shame for several reasons: because the abuser should be loving and protecting them, not hurting them; because the abuse goes on and on; and because sometimes it feels good (after all, the body is designed to respond to sexual stimulation). Children who are abused frequently grow up to distrust not only other people, but also themselves. Because of their feelings of distrust and fear about sex, developing healthy sexual relationships can be fraught with difficulties. It's not uncommon for children to suppress their memories of sexual abuse.

Sexual abuse relies on silence. Telling someone about the abuse, either a parent or teacher or trusted relative or friend, can have 2 positive effects: it destroys the abuser's power, and it paves the way for healing. Kids who speak up feel less alone and helpless. They're also able to direct their anger away from themselves and life in general and onto the abuser. It can take years, but through therapy and hard work, people can heal their anger, put the sexual abuse behind them, and form long-term relationships that are safe and loving.

Finding help

In recent years people have become aware that sexual abuse is a widespread problem. In response, help is available at many locations, including hospitals, community centres, youth groups, schools, churches, and synagogues. Look in your phone book under Rape, or see Resources at the end of this book if you or someone you know is being abused.

Q: Is it risky to date an older guy? ♀

A: Just because a guy is older than you doesn't mean he's a bad person. But if you're thinking of dating someone who's more than a couple of years older, here are a few things to look out for:

↘ He may have already had many sexual relationships, which means there's a greater chance he's infected with a sexually transmitted infection.

↘ If he's more experienced than you are, he may expect or pressure you to do sexual things you're not ready for.

↘ Older guys generally have more access to drugs and alcohol than younger guys do. If he's drunk or high, or if you both are, you may find yourself in a sexual situation that you really don't want to be in. Date rapes often happen under the influence of drugs and alcohol.

↘ Some guys only date younger girls because they're unsuccessful with women their own age. Maybe they're too immature. If that's the case, are you sure you want to be with someone who's not as grown up as he should be? Other guys don't want a real relationship; they just want to bask in the admiration younger girls give them. Before you get too attached to an older boyfriend, think about what his real reasons are for wanting to date you.

Sexual Assault

When someone does something sexual to you that you didn't consent to, you're being sexually assaulted. This usually happens to girls and women, but it also frequently happens to boys and even sometimes to men. The perpetrator is almost always male, but there are cases of women committing sexual assault, usually against children, but sometimes against other adults.

Sexual assault is a crime. Reporting it and pressing charges sends the message to everyone—sexual predators, other victims, people who've heard about it but haven't experienced it—that forcing someone into a sexual situation won't be tolerated. For many victims, it's also part of the healing process. Accusing your attacker in public is one way of taking back control and getting on with your life.

The majority of sexual assaults involve a guy putting his penis into someone's vagina or anus (also known as rape), inserting fingers or objects into someone's vagina or anus, touching a woman's breasts or vulva, or forcing someone to perform oral sex. It's possible the guy is a stranger to his victim, but it's far more likely that the victim knows him and even has some kind of a relationship with him. The list of people who've committed sexual assault includes boyfriends, husbands, family members, friends, co-workers, friends of friends, neighbours, and acquaintances.

The aftershock

Most people are terrified their attacker will return, which is why it's important to immediately get to a safe place. Right after the assault, it's possible to become confused or hysterical, or the other extreme could happen, where you turn strangely cold and unemotional. It's not uncommon for people to blame themselves and feel guilty for what happened, but a growing number of victims feel incredibly angry that they were assaulted. Long-term feelings such as fearfulness, self-blame, depression, helplessness, and distrust can have a negative effect on future relationships (particularly sexual ones), job performance, and general enjoyment of life.

What you should do after being raped

As soon as your attacker is gone, make sure you're safe, either by locking your doors or going to a place where you feel completely protected. Call someone you trust—a close friend or family member—or call 999 or your local police station. Some cities in the U.K. have a rape crisis centre which can offer advice, information and support, and may even provide someone to go with you to the police station or hospital. You can find details of your nearest centre in the phone directory or by calling the Rape Crisis Federation. **See Resources.**

But sooner rather than later, even if you're not sure you want to press charges, you need to call the police to report the crime. If you want to press charges at a later date, it will help your case if there's a file on the incident. Also, having accurate statistics helps the police and other groups in their fight against sexual assault. Your experience becomes part of the ever-growing voice that refuses to accept sex crimes in our society.

Put on clean clothes if you want, but put the clothes you were wearing at the time of the assault into a bag to give to the police. If the assault took place at home, don't wash your

Avoiding assault

Like everyone, you want to move freely and confidently through the world. To do this, it's necessary to adopt strategies that will protect your safe passage:

1. Travel in groups as much as possible.

2. If you're alone and on foot, walk with a purposeful stride, always staying aware of what's going on around you. Try to wear clothes and shoes you can run in.

3. When you're out at night, stay in well-lit areas.

4. Don't let down your guard in the early morning. Assaults aren't uncommon between 5 and 7 a.m.

5. If a stranger's approach makes you nervous, run away or enter a shop or house. It's common for girls to ignore their suspicions because they're afraid of being wrong and looking stupid. But there's nothing stupid about taking precautions that might save you from being raped.

6. When you're out with a guy, communicate your boundaries clearly. At the first hint that he wants something more than you're willing to give, set him straight immediately.

7. If you've just met someone at a party or club, don't go back to his place or even take a ride in his car, especially if either of you is drunk or stoned. Take some time to get to know him first, preferably with other people present. If you're the one doing the driving, don't give rides to strangers, no matter how cute they are.

8. When you're on the road at night, keep your car doors locked. And don't stop if another car bumps yours, especially at a traffic light. Some predators use a phony car accident as a way of gaining access to victims.

9. Don't hitchhike.

10. Take a self-defence course. Even a few hours with an instructor will teach you how to be more aggressive. You'll also come away with a handful of practical ideas about how to fight off an attacker.

sheets or tidy up. Also, try not to wash or eat or drink or even go to the bathroom. At the hospital or health clinic, you'll be asked to recount what happened in detail. You'll also be given a physical examination where evidence will be collected from your body (semen, saliva, pubic hair, blood samples). The examination may be unpleasant, but it's essential to have evidence against your attacker if you're going to take him to court. Try to stay focused and determined. If you absolutely can't, you may feel stronger at a later date. According to the law, rape can be reported long after it has occurred. Call a rape crisis centre if you need advice about going to the police.

If you were raped, the possibility of pregnancy and sexually transmitted infections has to be dealt with right away. You'll probably be offered emergency contraception and antibiotics to fight infections, and possibly a medication that can prevent HIV (it must be taken within a few hours of being raped). At a later date, you'll need to get tested for infections that don't show up on a test immediately, including hepatitis B and HIV. To be sure you're free of HIV, you have to test negative 3 to 6 months after the attack. After the exam you may have the chance to meet with a sexual assault counsellor, if you haven't already met with one. Long-term counselling can be very helpful, even if at the time you don't think you've been traumatized by what's happened.

Our society isn't known for being supportive of victims of sexual crimes, though in the last decade a wider range of people have begun to take all forms of sexual assault more seriously. Despite this new support, friends and even family members may raise their eyebrows and wonder what you did to "deserve" it. Even the police and other members of the criminal justice system can behave in ways that suggest you were the one at fault. If you end up testifying in court, you'll find that your attacker's lawyer will do everything in his or her power to discredit you, not only as a victim, but as a person. But no matter what attitudes you face, remember that you didn't commit the crime, someone else did. Fortunately, people who blame the victim have become less influential. This is thanks to the development of networks where doctors, nurses, police officers, counsellors, and lawyers are being specially trained to deal with assault victims with sensitivity and compassion.

Surviving an attack

Predators like easy targets. There's a chance that if you make yourself a difficult target, your attacker will give up, usually out of fear of being caught.

1. Try to run away. Running away is the safest option.

2. If you're trapped, make as much noise as possible. Scream, shout, or blow a whistle. Always carry a rape alarm.

3. Try not to panic. If you see an opportunity to get away from your attacker by fighting back, go for it—the law says you're entitled to defend yourself with "reasonable force." If you do attack back, poke your fingers into his eyes, hard. Bite him. Kick with all your might. Or give him a solid punch in the testicles or throat.

Sexual Harassment

If someone shows a sexual interest in you by making frequent eye contact, hanging around, or asking you to a movie or party, you have the option of returning that person's interest or not. If you return it and things progress nicely, then everyone's happy. If you communicate clearly that the feelings aren't mutual, it should be end-of-story. Let's say the person doesn't take no for an answer and continues to pester you with displays of their infatuation. Now you're being sexually harassed. It's intrusive and a pain in the neck. Frequently it's embarrassing, humiliating, and even frightening. And it's illegal!

Sexual harassment is defined as continued unwanted sexual attention. It can be verbal or physical or both. It includes making lewd comments, giving compliments of a sexual nature, sexual teasing, leering, pressuring for dates, and making sounds or

Sexual harassment is illegal. If you're being sexually harassed

↘ be clear about the behaviour that upsets you;

↘ describe the upsetting behaviour to the person who's doing it and ask him or her to stop (it's a good idea to have a friend or adult with you to act as a witness and as support);

↘ if the harassment continues, write down on paper when and where the offending behaviour took place;

↘ complain to someone in a position of authority and show what you've written, then, if the person in authority doesn't take action, go to a higher authority, even the police;

↘ as a last resort, take legal action if possible (this takes time, money, and courage, but in the end it can be worth it).

Speaking out against sexual harassment, and sometimes prosecuting, tells offenders that their behaviour is unacceptable and that they can't get away with it. It also offers a positive example to others who are too insecure or frightened to speak out themselves. Many people don't realize that their comments or gestures are actually sexual harassment. How will they know unless you tell them?

gestures that suggest sexual activity. It also includes standing too close and uninvited grabbing, touching, kissing, and hugging. Cases of sexual harassment that are more subtle often involve older people in positions of authority, for example, a PE teacher who keeps his pupils in line by making sneering comments about their anatomy.

Given that we live in a world shaped by hierarchies where men have more power, it's not surprising that sexual harassment happens more often to women than to men. The most common kind is "hostile environment" sexual harassment. This is when a specific location—your school, a park, the place where you work, the local swimming pool—is uncomfortable to be in because there are pornographic pictures or obscene graffiti, or because people talk loudly about tits, cocks, sluts, bitches, studs, fags, or queens. This type of environment reduces people to sex objects.

Sexual Intercourse

↘ shagging ↘ humping
↘ screwing ↘ bonking
↘ coitus ↘ having sex
↘ fucking
↘ sleeping together
↘ making love
↘ copulating
↘ fornication

Almost everyone uses the term sexual inter-course to describe penis-vagina sex. In the old days, this activity fell under strict societal guidelines—intercourse outside of marriage was bad, intercourse inside of marriage was good. This had a lot to do with the centuries-old religious belief that sex was for reproduc-tion only. In recent decades, religious beliefs have had less influence on society, and guide-lines about intercourse have become relaxed. Nowadays, the onus is on individuals to know what they think and feel about sex and to make up their own minds about when to have it. This period of decision-making might be a good time to take the focus off intercourse—for the main reason that avoiding penetration decreases the chance of pregnancy and contracting a sexually transmitted infection. Enjoying sexual intimacy with a partner can involve a wide

Q & A

Q: Why do people use slang so much when they talk about sex?

A: Everyone is sexual, so when people talk about sex, there's always a personal involvement, even when they're just joking around. Slang is one way to make sex less personal. By using slang, which is often funny, people feel less uncomfortable or embarrassed when they talk about sex.

Q: ♂ The last time my girlfriend and I had sex, she asked me to stop because my penis was hurting her. Was I doing something wrong?

A: If you're asking if there was something wrong with your thrusting, probably not, unless you were being very rough. If you were just doing the usual sensitive in-and-out, there are 2 likely reasons why your girlfriend felt pain: her vagina wasn't lubricated, or the muscles in her vagina weren't relaxed. Either way, she wasn't ready for sex. Next time you and your girlfriend plan to have sex, make sure she really wants to do it. Also, put aside enough time for slow, sensual foreplay. Good foreplay should make her aroused. If your girlfriend continues to have pain despite good foreplay, she should see a doctor to make sure she doesn't have an infection.

STIs you can get

- HIV
- herpes
- genital warts
- gonorrhoea
- chlamydia
- syphilis
- hepatitis A, B, and C
- trichomoniasis
- crabs
- scabies
- intestinal parasites
- molluscum contagiosum

Some girls think they won't get pregnant if they stand upright after having sex. Not true. No matter what position you're in, as soon as sperm touches your vagina, it races toward the fallopian tubes, hoping to find an egg to fertilize.

range of fun-filled, sexy, sensual activities that don't include actual intercourse.

People start having intercourse for lots of reasons: to find out what sex is really like, to lose their virginity, to express deep love in a committed relationship, to prove their manhood or woman-hood, to dispel personal insecurities, for the thrill of it, to feel part of the adult world, to keep a relationship going, because everyone else is doing it, and so on. If you're still a virgin, when do you think you'll start having sex? Why will you start? If you're already having intercourse, why are you doing it? Are you satisfied with the other ways that you and your partner express your sexual feelings?

Intercourse is the number 1 way that HIV is spread from infected men to women. At present, 90% of all new HIV infections are the result of this kind of sex. Over 15 other sexually transmitted infections are also transmitted during intercourse, and some of them are incurable. Despite the reality of infection and disease, people are still regularly having intercourse. Wisely, many of them are protecting themselves against pregnancy and STIs. The best way to do this is to use a condom with a birth control method such as the Pill or Implanon (a hormonal implant). While protection is never 100% effective, this type of combination method comes very close.

In many cases, protection is still a good idea even if you're in a monogamous relationship. One of you may be infected from a previous relationship and not know it because there are no symptoms. Also, you or your partner could have an affair outside the relationship, then feel too guilty or unconcerned about it to say anything. Even a one-night stand can bring an infection into your relationship.

Sexuality

Everyone has sexual feelings, whether or not they're aware of them. Babies love to be held and stroked. Toddlers play with their genitals. Young children have fantasies infused with mysterious sensuality. In puberty, children become adolescents who are newly conscious of sexual thoughts, sensations, and emotions. As teenagers, they become increasingly sexually attracted to people around them. They feel desire, and sooner or later have their first sexual encounters. They fall in love and develop intimate relation-ships. Some people have children. Throughout life, old relationships are maintained and new ones are formed. The body continues to feel desire, though by now the desire may have become less intense. All of this is sexuality. Like the air we breathe, sexuality pervades every part of life.

Sexual Orientation

Secondary school was probably the setting of your first romance. There was that girl or boy you really, really liked. As the years passed you had more crushes and a few infatuations. Maybe you fell in love with a neighbour, a best friend, or the person who sat next to you in school. Who were the objects of your desire? Boys? Girls? Boys and girls? Because we live in a world dominated by heterosexual love, if you were a girl who liked boys, or a boy who liked girls, you probably didn't think much of it. But if you were a girl who was attracted again and again to girls, eventually you became aware that your sexual orientation was different than almost everyone else's. If you were a boy who was consistently attracted to boys, you faced the same truth: your sexual orientation was different. Little did you know there were others around you experiencing the same feelings. Or that some of your friends and classmates were quietly confused by the fact that sometimes they liked boys, and other times, girls were far more exciting.

Sexual orientation is something people become increasingly aware of as they move through their teen years and into their twenties. Many people know with certainty at an early age which sex they prefer. Many others only discover their sexual identity over several years and after some experimentation. A growing number of people resist the pressure to commit to a particular orientation. Uncomfortable with the limitations demanded by traditional labels (straight, gay, lesbian, bisexual) they prefer the openness offered by queer love. See Queer.

Q: What if I lose my erection when I put on a condom?

A: Throw the condom away, get your erection back, and slip on a new condom. It will be easier to stay hard if you and your friend make putting on a condom part of your sex play. Or you can practise at home while you're masturbating.

Smegma

This is a thick, whitish substance that looks a bit like cottage cheese.

In females ♀

Smegma acts as a lubricant between the clitoris and the hood, allowing the hood to move easily back and forth over the clitoris. It also collects between the labia minora. If you don't rinse it away regularly with warm water, it can cause irritation.

In males ♂

Smegma is secreted from the head of the penis as a lubricant, allowing the foreskin easy movement over the head. If it gathers too long under the foreskin it can become foul-smelling and might lead to infection. Guys who are circumcised don't have to worry about the accumulation of smegma, but if you're uncircumcised, you should wash under your foreskin with warm water every few days to clear it away.

Sperm carry the chromosomes that determine the sex of the baby.

Sperm ♂

Starting in puberty, millions of male sex cells are made in the testicles every day—according to one report, up to 50,000 per minute! These are called sperm. As they travel through tubes in the scrotum, sperm mix with other fluids to become semen.

Whether you like it or not, the function of your sperm is to get your girlfriend pregnant. If semen is ejaculated inside or near her vagina, sperm will quickly swim up the vagina, through the cervix, through the uterus and into the fallopian tubes. The first one to pierce the egg is the winner. So unless you're ready to become a dad, keep your sperm under wraps. Wear a condom.

Spermicides

Spermicides are chemical products that are inserted deep into the vagina before intercourse. Their job is to kill sperm. Conveniently, they also kill other organisms, including the bacteria that cause chlamydia and gonorrhoea. Spermicides can be purchased in several forms—foam, jelly, cream, suppository, film, and tablet—though not all of these are available in every chemist. Each form has specific instructions about where to put it, when to use it, and how much to use. Because of this variety, when you choose a spermicide, make sure you read the instructions carefully to know exactly what to do.

A spermicide is a good purchase if you're planning to use it with a condom, diaphragm, or cervical cap. Used alone, it's less than 80% effective in preventing pregnancy, but when used with a condom, the number rises to 97%. When used with a diaphragm or cervical cap, spermicides are just over 90% effective. For maximum protection, all spermicides must be left in the vagina for 6 to 8 hours after sex. Also, new spermicide must be inserted before each act of intercourse. Condoms can be purchased that already have a coating of spermicide, usually Nonoxynol-9. The contraceptive sponge also contains spermicide.

Unfortunately, the agent in most spermicides, Nonoxynol-9, can cause irritation or an allergic reaction in some users. Women should watch for unusual discharge, tenderness or a rash in the vaginal area, a sore or blister near or in the genitals or anus, discomfort or a burning sensation during urination, and pain during intercourse. Men should look for the same symptoms, including a discharge from their penis, but excluding pain during intercourse. In both sexes, frequent urination can also be a symptom of an allergy.

Advantages

The only birth control method besides the condom that protects against some STIs. Gives women control over contraception. Adding it to the vagina only takes 20 to 30 seconds. Sold over the counter at chemists. Not very expensive. Provides extra lubrication during sex.

Disadvantages

Not very effective when used alone. Each brand has specific instructions, which must be read carefully before use. Nonoxynol-9, the killing agent in most spermicides, can cause irritation and itchiness in the vulva and penis. One study showed that frequent use of Nonoxynol-9 can create sores that allow infections such as HIV to enter the body more easily. Can lead to yeast or urinary tract infections in women. Tastes bad, which puts a damper on oral sex. Must be put in just before sex, interrupting spontaneity. Can be messy.

Availability

Most chemist shops carry a good variety of brands.

Q: Does Nonoxynol-9 protect against the virus that causes AIDS?

A: For a long time people thought that it did. However, recent studies prove that spermicides with Nonoxynol-9 don't protect against HIV. In fact, the repeated use of Nonoxynol-9 may cause sores in the vaginal area that make it easier for the virus to enter the body.

Q: Do spermicides cause cancer?

A: Spermicides don't cause cancer. In fact, they may help prevent cancer of the cervix.

Q: Can I use a spermicide if I have my period?

A: There's no harm in using spermicides during menstruation, but because they'll flow out of the body along with the menstrual fluid, they'll be less effective.

Condoms used with spermicides offer excellent protection against pregnancy and most STIs.

Sponge ♀

↘contraceptive sponge

As a method of birth control, the sponge sounds interesting—it sits in the vagina in front of the cervix and traps sperm, then kills them—but unless it's used with a condom, it isn't very effective. Used perfectly, it works around 90% of the time, unless you've given birth, in which case it works less well. In combination with a condom, its effectiveness rises to 98%. Made of dense white foam, the sponge destroys sperm because it contains 3 different spermicides. It protects against pregnancy over several hours and must be kept in for at least 6 hours after intercourse. When its job is done, the sponge is removed and thrown away.

Advantages

The 3 spermicides do battle against some germs, including the bacteria that cause chlamydia and gonorrhoea. Can't be felt by either partner. One size fits all. Easy to put in and take out, though some practice is necessary. Inexpensive. Easy to carry. Can be purchased over the counter.

Disadvantages

Not very effective on its own. The spermicides may cause an allergic reaction. Because you can't feel it, the sponge can be forgotten in the vagina, which could lead to toxic shock syndrome. Can be messy.

Availability

There is no sponge currently available in the U.K. For commercial reasons, the last brand, Protectaid, has been withdrawn. However, the Today sponge, or another brand using a different spermicide, might well be reintroduced.

STDs
↘ **sexually transmitted diseases**

For the past few decades people have used the term STDs to refer to infections that are transmitted through sexual contact. More recently, a new term is being used, STIs, which stands for sexually transmitted infections. Some people feel that STIs, with its emphasis on infections, is a more accurate and sympathetic description than STDs, which emphasizes diseases. When referring to infections that are passed from one person to another as a result of sexual activity, this book uses the newer label, sexually transmitted infections, or STIs. See STIs.

Stereotypes

People often form impressions about other people based on sex, religion, ethnic background, or nationality. These impressions are communicated to others in a variety of ways—by word of mouth, in jokes and textbooks, through the media or advertising. When enough people share the same impression, a stereotype is born. Soon the stereotype takes on a life of its own, even to the point of perpetuating stereotypical behaviour. For example, overweight men and women are often perceived as being non-sexual, so many of them begin to feel that way.

Stereotypes are also used to make assumptions about new acquaintances. Who people are as individuals isn't taken into account. This can be hurtful and demeaning, not to mention harmful to the well-being of the people who are being stereotyped. You probably believe in a few stereotypes. Do you know what they are?

Sexual stereotypes

The following statements are all powerful sexual stereotypes that have damaging consequences. Despite the fact that each one is false, many people believe these stereotypes to be true.

↘ Women are less sexual than men.
↘ Men are sexual predators.
↘ "Macho" guys can keep an erection going forever.
↘ Girls with large breasts are "easy."
↘ Boys with big penises are studs.

Sterilization

Women and men who are certain they don't want children, or don't want more children, can undergo sterilization, which is a surgical procedure that makes people infertile. The procedure for women is tubal ligation; for men, vasectomy. Sterilization almost guarantees that intercourse won't result in pregnancy. Because it's usually permanent, sterilization isn't recommended for teenagers, who may not be prepared to make a decision that has such long-term consequences. Sterilization doesn't protect against STIs.

In females

In a tubal ligation, the 2 fallopian tubes are disconnected from the uterus, which means the eggs can't meet incoming sperm. No fertilization = no pregnancy. However, the ovaries continue to produce eggs, which are eventually absorbed by the body. The menstrual cycle is unchanged, and most women report that their desire for sex is also unchanged.

In males

In a vasectomy, the 2 tubes (the vas deferens) that transport the sperm to the urethra are severed. Ejaculation is still possible, but the semen won't contain any sperm. No sperm = no pregnancy. The sperm that remain in the body are absorbed by the surrounding tissue. The force of the ejaculation is unchanged, and the ejaculate even looks the same as if it were filled with sperm. Most men report that libido is also unchanged.

STIs
↘sexually transmitted infections

In a T.V. advert an attractive teenage girl casually describes herpes as being a hassle. She's right. Herpes is a virus that won't go away, but it's manageable. Another virus that's even more manageable, but still aggravating, is molluscum contagiosum. Symptoms can hang around for a few years, but you won't suffer anything worse than several patches of sore skin and possible embarrassment if the bumps are visible.

Other viruses that are transmitted through sexual contact and aren't so manageable include genital warts, which may indicate the presence of cancerous cells in the cervix, and HIV, which leads to AIDS. Fortunately, early detection of genital warts is possible through regular cervical smears and the treatment for cancerous cells is often effective. While there's still no cure for HIV, drug treatments are prolonging the lives of many people with the virus. Hepatitis A, B, and C are also viral infections for which there's no cure, though a vaccine is available for A and B. The good thing about hepatitis is that in the majority of people who are infected, the body creates an immunity, so once the symptoms subside, they don't return. The problem is that the people who don't develop an immunity become carriers of the virus and over time develop permanent liver damage. Carriers can also infect others.

Some sexually transmitted infections are caused by bacteria. Among these are chlamydia, gonorrhoea, and syphilis, which are all easily cured with antibiotics. Untreated, however, they can lead to extremely unpleasant diseases where fertility or

Self-examination

If you're sexually active—kissing, masturbating your partner, having intercourse, participating in anal or oral sex—there's something you can do besides going for regular testing. Do self-examinations. Look for lumps, bumps, sores, and unusual discharge. If you detect something, stop having sex until you visit a doctor to find out what it is. If you're diagnosed with an infection, tell previous partners what you've got so they can get treated too. Because some STIs are difficult to deal with on your own, confide in someone you trust. Talking can really help. See Confidentiality, Testing.

The more partners you have, the greater your risk of catching a sexually transmitted infection.

GET TESTED

You may be
infected but
don't know it
because:

↘the symptoms
haven't shown
up yet

↘the symptoms
are so mild
you don't
notice them

↘the symptoms
are in hard-
to-see places

↘you're one
of a number
of people who
won't get the
symptoms

↘the symptoms
came, then
went away,
so you thought
you weren't
infected.

STIs

eyesight is lost, and in the case of syphilis, where
insanity is followed by death. Bacterial vaginosis, also
caused by bacteria, is far less serious. Fortunately, it
can be successfully treated with antibiotics.

Three less harmful but still annoying STIs
are actually parasites. They include pubic lice, scabies,
and trichomoniasis (trich for short). Transmitted
through skin-to-skin contact, these infections can be
stopped upon diagnosis—pubic lice and scabies by
killing them with pesticides, trich by taking antibiotics.
Last but not least, yeast infections plague millions of
women and some men, but only temporarily if treated
carefully with an anti-fungal cream.

Women are more at risk

Women catch many sexually transmitted infections more easily
than men do. This is because the vagina, with its several inches
of mucous membrane, offers a bigger area that can be infected
than the penis, which is mostly skin. Also, STIs that are carried
in semen and vaginal fluids can be found in large amounts in
semen, but much smaller amounts in vaginal fluid. Finally, the
act of penis-vagina sex can cause tiny cuts in the fragile skin
of the vagina, making it easier for germs to pass into the body.
It doesn't help that semen is squirted into the vagina with
some force and that it stays there even after sex is over.

The stigma

Many people feel embarrassed or ashamed to discover they
have a sexually transmitted infection. Others are convinced
they're being punished for indulging their sexual desire. It's
not uncommon for victims to feel unclean, as if these infections
were somehow worse than the flu or bronchitis. No one feels
guilty about catching the measles. Then why do people have such
negative reactions when they find out they have a sexually

transmitted infection? Because of the words "sexually transmitted." After thousands of years of existence, people are still judging each other for being sexually active.

The negative aura that surrounds sexually transmitted infections has a dangerous consequence: feeling humiliated, people often don't seek testing or treatment. As a result, infections that can be cured in a matter of days or weeks are undetected or ignored. Over time they turn into diseases that cause serious and sometimes permanent damage to the body. As infected people go about their daily lives, the infections continue to spread. For anyone having sex, the answer to this problem is to ignore the stigma and make regular testing a part of your health care, even if you're having safer sex. Most people will agree that this is sensible. What do you think?

Syphilis

For centuries, syphilis was one of the most dreaded diseases on the planet. Transmitted through sexual contact, it ravaged people's bodies and minds and eventually left them dead. Today, syphilis is an infection that's rarely seen and easily cured. If you know you have it and get treatment, it can be gone after a single shot of antibiotics. It's even curable in its late stage, but by then irreversible damage may have been done to your body.

The symptoms of syphilis show up in 3 stages, though many people don't notice the stage-1 symptom because it develops somewhere that's hard to see, such as on the cervix or inside the anus. Some people never get symptoms.

Stage 1:

Nine to 90 days after infection, a small, round, painless sore (called a chancre, pronounced SHANK-er) appears on the skin where contact was made with an infected person. Because contact usually means intercourse, anal sex, oral sex, or kissing,

Chancres

♀ In females

Chancres most commonly develop inside the vagina, on the cervix, and on the vaginal lips. They can also pop up around the anus, in the rectum, in and around the mouth, and near the nipple.

♂ In males

Look for a chancre to develop on the tip of your penis near the urethra, on the edge of the head, along the shaft, or on the scrotum. Chancres can also show up around the anus, in the rectum, and in or around the mouth.

Getting tested

If you discover a sore you suspect is a chancre, make an appointment with a doctor for a diagnosis. At your appointment, your symptoms will be noted and a sample of the fluid from the chancre may be examined, though this is uncommon. A better way to test for syphilis is to have a blood test 4 weeks after the chancre first appeared. Ask your partner to go in for a diagnosis too.

Syphilis

Syphilis

Treatment

One shot of penicillin should do the trick, though in some cases a second or third dose is needed. Your doctor will ask you to provide a few blood tests over the coming year to make sure the syphilis has been eliminated from your body. Don't be sexually intimate with anyone until you're told with certainty that the bacteria are gone.

Prevention

Don't get physically close to someone who has a chancre sore or skin rash. Using a condom doesn't offer protection from the rash because it can be so extensive, in some cases covering the whole body. A good way to prevent the permanent damage caused by late-stage syphilis is to have regular testing just to make sure you don't have the bacteria.

the chancre almost always appears in or around the genitals, anus, or mouth. A skin rash may or may not develop somewhere else on the body. If no rash develops and the chancre is hidden inside the vagina or anus, the syphilis goes undetected and untreated. After a few weeks both the chancre and rash disappear, but the bacteria continue to move through the body.

Stage 2:

A month or 2 later, new symptoms show up, including one or more of the following: sore throat, sores in the mouth, aching muscles, fever, fatigue, hair loss, and small growths on the genitals. Some people develop a rash that covers their entire body, though in others, the rash concentrates on the hands and feet. After a few months these symptoms disappear. People who attribute them to the flu miss being diagnosed and treated for syphilis. As before, the bacteria continue to move through the body. Some people never have further symptoms. People who get further symptoms may have to wait years, even decades, for them to show up.

Stage 3:

This is also known as late-stage syphilis. By now the bacteria have caused significant damage throughout the body. In one third of people with syphilis, one or more of the following symptoms may show up: blindness, deafness, skin ulcers, heart disease, liver damage, paralysis, and insanity. For many victims, this stage ends in death.

Syphilis is a type of bacteria that lives in the bloodstream of people who are infected. To contract the bacteria, it's necessary to have direct skin contact with someone who's already infected. Your skin must touch that person's rash or chancre, which is highly contagious when it oozes liquid. During contact, the bacteria enter your body through mucous membranes in your vagina, anus, or mouth, or through tiny cracks in your skin. Syphilis is most contagious during stages 1 and 2. After 1 year without symptoms, the disease is no longer contagious, though a pregnant woman can pass the infection to her unborn child at any time. See Chancre.

Q: Will I lose my virginity if I put a tampon in my vagina?

A: No, though if you have a hymen, you may stretch it. The only ways to lose your virginity are through penis-vagina intercourse (heterosexual sex) or by reaching orgasm during sexual activity with another woman (lesbian sex).

Q: How old do I have to be before I can use tampons?

A: You can start using tampons with your first period, though it might be wise to wait until you've had a few periods so you can be a better judge of your flow. When using tampons, it's extremely important to use the right size for the amount of flow you have.

Q: Is it possible for a tampon to go through my vagina and get lost inside my body?

A: Never. The end of the vagina has a hole in it that leads to the cervix, but the hole is much too small for a tampon to pass through. A tampon goes in through the vaginal opening and has to come out the same way.

Tampons ♀
↘plugs

Many women heaved a sigh of relief when commercial tampons became available in the 1930s. Tampons fit neatly into the vagina to soak up menstrual flow. They were discreet, easy to take out, and quick to dispose of. There was no mess and no odour. They were convenient. Decades later, millions of women still use tampons to deal with their menstrual flow. But not everyone starts out using tampons. In fact, when most girls first get their periods, they use sanitary towels for months or even years. They only move on to tampons when they feel more comfortable with their bodies or they can't resist the convenience any longer. Despite the improvements made to pads over the years, tampons still offer a better solution to the problem posed by swimming during menstruation.

Not everyone thinks tampons are a good thing. Some women are concerned by the fact that most tampons are manufactured with chlorine-bleached cotton, which may release toxins into the body (non-chlorine-bleached tampons can be found at some health food shops). Also, tampons that aren't used correctly can lead to toxic shock syndrome, a rare disease that can be fatal. Other women are disturbed by the staggering volume of used tampons and applicators that are dumped at landfill sites every year. They encourage a return to reusable cloth pads, though much funkier ones than their grandmothers used. Other women advocate a relatively new product called the Keeper, which catches menstrual flow in a small cup. See Keeper, Sanitary Towels, Toxic Shock Syndrome.

How to use tampons

Chemists usually stock a variety of sizes, from slim to regular to super-absorbent. Make sure you choose the least absorbent tampon for your flow. Every box of tampons comes with detailed instructions about how to insert them. Helpful diagrams are usually included. Some instruction sheets also contain information on toxic shock syndrome and how to avoid it. Read these instructions carefully before attempting to put in your first tampon. Most of all, pay attention to the diagram of the vagina. Notice that it's on a slant, which means you don't push straight up when you're putting a tampon in, but toward the base of your spine. And try to be relaxed. When it's in, check to see that the string is hanging out.

Safety tips

➥ Don't choose a size that's too absorbent for your flow. For example, a tampon should be so wet that it easily slips out of the vagina when the string is pulled. One that's too absorbent will make the vagina dry. Anyone who's ever pulled a tampon out of a dry vagina knows how unpleasant it feels. Use a slim tampon or sanitary pad on light days, a regular-size tampon on medium-flow days, and a super-absorbent tampon only when your menstrual flow is very heavy.

➥ Wash your hands before putting a tampon in.

➥ Tampons need to be changed every 4 to 6 hours. If possible, alternate between tampons and pads.

➥ Remove the used tampon before inserting a new one.

➥ Don't go to bed at night with a tampon in. Most manufacturers of sanitary towels make extra-long pads for overnight use.

➥ If you prefer to use an applicator, use the cardboard kind instead of the plastic kind. Plastic applicators can cause tiny tears in the vagina, not to mention the fact that they create more rubbish, contributing to the landfill problem. Many people find it simpler just to use their finger.

➥ Don't use perfumed tampons, which can irritate the vagina.

➥ A tampon that feels uncomfortable may not be in far enough. Either push it in with your finger, or take it out and try again with a new tampon.

Q & A ♀

Q: I put a tampon in and now I can't find it!

A: It's possible for a tampon to move deep into the vagina and get stuck near the back. Reach in with your index or middle finger and try to manoeuvre it toward the vaginal opening. If you're not successful, ask your partner or a friend to help. As a last resort go to a doctor, hospital or health clinic, where a nurse or doctor will find the tampon and remove it. If you don't get it out, it won't be long before your vagina starts to smell. There's also a very small risk of developing toxic shock syndrome.

Tampons must be removed before intercourse.

Q&A
Q: Why does one of my balls hang lower than the other?

A: Most guys have one ball that hangs a bit lower, and there's a reason for it. Each testicle hangs by a cord. Usually, one cord is longer than the other so that the testicles don't bang against each other when a guy walks or runs. Instead they slide by each other.

Teasing

When you establish power over someone by turning that person on sexually, then walking away, you're being a tease. This isn't the same as flirting, which is a playful, no-strings-attached way of communicating sexually with someone you like. It's also not the same as leaving a sexual situation because it's gone too far and you feel uncomfortable. Teasing is manipulative and may or may not include a put-down. It usually leaves the other person feeling confused, hurt, or angry. People who are guilty of teasing usually deny it. Sometimes people are unfairly accused of being teases when they decide they've reached their limit and say no to sex.

Testicles ♂

↘balls   ↘nuts   ↘cobblers
↘family jewels   ↘bollocks
↘testes   ↘gonads   ↘nads

Just behind the penis is a sac of skin called the scrotum. Inside the scrotum, nestled side by side, are the 2 highly sensitive male sex glands. These are the testicles. A lot of important activity goes on in the testicles. Significant amounts of testosterone are produced there. Sperm are also produced. As soon as the sperm are formed, they begin their journey through the testicles' various chambers and tubes. Finally they combine with other fluids to make semen.

Even though most boys spend more time getting to know their penis than their testicles, they're not unfamiliar with what hangs inside their sacs. For example, many boys are aware that their testes sometimes change position. When it's hot out, the testes stay cool by hanging away from the body. In cold weather, or in chilly water, they pull in as close as possible for warmth. This happens because the production of sperm can only take place at a particular temperature. During moments of fright, the testicles draw back in hopes of protecting the precious sperm.

Undescended testicles

A small percentage of boys are born with empty scrotums. They have testicles, but the testicles are still in the abdominal cavity, where they developed. They should have fallen into the scrotum a short time before birth, but for some reason didn't. Boys in this predicament have what's called undescended testicles. Sometimes the testicles "descend" just after birth or several months later. Some boys have only one undescended testicle. If a boy's 2 testicles haven't descended by the age of 6, his chances of developing testicular cancer almost double. In many cases, undescended testicles can be corrected by hormone treatment or surgery.

Torsion of the testicles

Inside the scrotum, each testicle hangs by a cord. It can happen that the cord gets twisted, cutting off the blood supply. The pain is immediate and severe. Sometimes the scrotum swells and turns blue. If the cord isn't untwisted the testicle will die. See a doctor immediately if you experience a sudden, very sharp pain in your testicle that doesn't go away after a few minutes.

Testicular self-examination

Testicular cancer begins with a small lump that develops on the side of one testicle, though sometimes it can be found on the front. To catch the lump before it grows, check your testicles every month after you turn 15. Examining your testicles only takes a couple of minutes. If you already feel yourself there from time to time, all you need to do is add a bit of technique and focus. It will be easier to feel the lump if your scrotum is relaxed, so do the examination after a warm bath or shower. Testicular cancer is the most common cancer in teenage males. Fortunately, it has a very high cure rate when caught early.

Self-examination ♂

1. Using both hands, examine each testicle one at a time.

2. Place the index and middle fingers of both hands under your right testicle. Your thumbs should be resting on top of the testicle, tips nearly touching. Very gently roll the testicle between the fingers and thumbs. This shouldn't hurt. Now do the left testicle.

3. The lump that stretches from the top of the testicle down the back is the epididymis, which is one of the tubes that carry the sperm. Otherwise, the testicle should feel smooth and firm.

Either before or after examining yourself with your fingers, take a few minutes to check your testicles in the mirror. Look for swelling on the scrotum. Another sign of cancer is a sudden shrinking of one of the testicles.

↘screening

There are over a dozen different sexually transmitted infections described in this book. Some of them are so widespread, there's a substantial chance you'll catch one during the years you're sexually active. If this happens, you may not realize you're infected. As a result, you won't get treated and the infection could spread through your body or you could pass it on to new partners. Going for regular testing can help you minimize these problems. Once diagnosed, you can manage the infection and in some cases even eliminate it. Tests are available for most STIs, but not all clinics offer them. Ask your doctor what's available at your clinic and where you can go for testing that isn't readily available.

STI testing doesn't always produce reliable results. Even HIV tests are only accurate 99.9% of the time. When cultures are sent to labs, it's possible to get a negative result when you're positive, or a positive result when you're negative. If you have reason not to trust your test result, get tested again.

If you're a guy without symptoms, it may be particularly hard to get an accurate result. A sample that's taken from just inside the tip of your penis won't show germs that are living further down the urethra. For the most accurate results, don't urinate for 4 hours before the test as urination can flush out the bacteria that's needed for testing. Sometimes your best clue to your health status is the health of your partner. If she or he has an infection such as chlamydia, gonorrhoea, herpes, or genital warts, assume that you have it too and go for treatment. See Confidentiality.

Recommendations

Get tested on your own or with your partner:

↘ once a year if you're in a steady relationship and practising safer sex
↘ twice a year if you have numerous partners and are practising safer sex
↘ after each new partner if you've had unprotected sex

Check with your doctor to find out how long you need to wait before testing will show accurate results, for example, it takes 2 to 3 weeks for gonorrhoea and chlamydia germs to show up, and 3 to 6 months for HIV antibodies to be present in the bloodstream.

Where to go

↘ your family doctor
↘ community youth centres (there's often someone on hand who knows about sex-related issues)
↘ your local GU medicine or sexual health clinic
↘ your school nurse
↘ student health services at a university campus or college

What to expect

Depending on what you're being tested for, the doctor or nurse will:

- ask about your medical and sexual history
- ask for a urine sample
- take a blood sample
- take a swab from your throat, rectum, urethra, or all 3
- give you an internal pelvic examination (female)
- examine your genitals and surrounding skin
- examine your testicles (male)

Toxic Shock Syndrome ♀

TSS

This is a rare and very serious disease that occurs primarily in menstruating women. It's caused by bacteria that build up in the vagina and eventually produce toxins in the body. The symptoms include sudden high fever, vomiting, diarrhoea, aching muscles, dizziness, low blood pressure, and a red skin rash. Women who experience these symptoms while using a tampon, diaphragm, cervical cap, or sponge should remove the object from their vagina, go to the nearest hospital casualty department and ask for immediate attention. For some women, toxic shock syndrome has ended in death.

Many researchers believe that toxic shock syndrome is linked to the way tampons are used. For example, a tampon should be so soaked with blood that it easily slips out of the vagina when the string is pulled. This can only happen if the tampon isn't too absorbent for the menstrual flow. A tampon that's too absorbent will make the vagina dry. Also, the friction of the tampon against the vaginal walls may cause small tears that allow bacteria into the body. To avoid all this, a slim tampon or sanitary towel should be used on light days, a regular-size tampon should be used when there's a medium amount of flow,

Toxic Shock Syndrome ♀

Treatment

Your doctor will prescribe antibiotics.

Prevention

For many women, tampons are too convenient to give up altogether. If that's the case with you, the trick is to use the right size of tampon for the amount of flow you have. For some women, this means never using the super-absorbent kind. To find out how to use tampons safely, see Tampons.

and a super-absorbent tampon should only be used on days when the menstrual flow is very heavy. .

Another problem with tampon use is that sometimes they're left in the vagina for too long. Tampons should be changed every 4 to 6 hours. If possible, a sanitary towel should be used for short periods between taking out one tampon and putting in another. It's never advised to wear a tampon through the night. Sponges should be removed after 12 hours, and diaphragms and cervical caps shouldn't be left in the vagina for longer than 24 hours. See Tampons.

Transgendered

Some people are born with the anatomy of one sex, but throughout their entire lives, beginning as early as ages 5 or 6, identify with the opposite gender. A woman with breasts and a vagina may in fact feel very male. Identifying as a man, she's very comfortable when expressing her maleness. Likewise, a man with testicles and a penis may feel most at ease when expressing his female self. People who decide to change their biological sex to match their gender identity are known as transsexuals. Those who decide not to have a "sex-change operation" (the process of "transitioning"), call themselves transgendered. Even though they identify with the opposite gender, they're comfortable with their sexual anatomy and don't feel the need to make any changes.

How a transgendered man or woman expresses sexual love is entirely individual: a woman who identifies as a man may love men or women, though it's more likely she/he will love women, and a man who identifies as a woman may love women or men, though it's more likely he/she will love men. Transgendered behaviour can also include bisexuality. Due to pressures to conform to traditional gender roles, coming to terms with being transgendered can be a long and difficult journey. The support of family and friends is extremely helpful, but when that fails, most cities have welcoming networks that offer reassurance and advice. See Queer, Transsexual.

Transsexual

This is a person who has the anatomy of one sex, but identifies totally with the other sex. For example, take a guy by the name of Jo Bloggs, who's a physically healthy male in every way. The problem is, Jo feels like a female trapped in a male body. These feelings started in early childhood, when he was 5 or 6, and they were very strong. To get relief from his dilemma, Jo imagined himself as a girl. Later he found comfort in dressing like a girl. By adulthood, Jo was cross-dressing regularly, not to find sexual excitement, but because it felt right.

More than anything, Jo wishes the world would treat him like the woman he believes he is. With this goal in mind, he decides to have a "sex-change operation." This is actually a much longer process than one operation, and is called "transitioning" by those who go through it. Transitioning is time-consuming, expensive, and irreversible, but the vast majority of people who've done it report satisfaction with their new life. People with gender issues like Jo's who don't feel the need to change their sexual anatomy through surgery are often not considered to be transsexual, but transgendered.

Transsexuals can be male-to-female, like Jo, or female-to-male. In terms of love, some desire to be part of heterosexual relationships, while others only form gay or lesbian relationships. Some are attracted to both sexes. Regardless of sexual orientation, most transsexuals face many difficult challenges on their road to becoming comfortable in their own bodies. Networks of support groups offer valuable help. See Queer, Transgendered.

Treatment

Your doctor will prescribe antibiotics. While you're taking them, don't have sex with anyone. When the antibiotics are finished, the trich will be gone. It's important to have your partner treated at the same time so you don't become re-infected the next time you have sex together. Also, remember to call your previous partners to warn them that they may be infected.

Prevention

The best protection from these unwelcome parasites is to use a condom whenever you have sex. Also, avoid wearing other people's underwear or bathing suits, and don't dry yourself with a towel that's just been used by someone else. You don't want your genitals to come into contact with fluids that may contain trich.

Q & A

Q: Will I become immune to trich once I've had it?

A: There's no immunity to trich. You can catch it again and again.

Trichomoniasis
↘trich

This infection is caused by tiny parasites that make their home in warm, moist places in the human body, particularly the vagina. In fact, thousands of human bodies across the United Kingdom are home to these nasty little bugs. Because they can live for several hours in body fluids that have been left on clothing, bed sheets, or a towel, it's possible to become infected by putting your genitals in contact with these fluids. However, most cases of trich are transmitted from one person to another by sexual intercourse and vulva-to-vulva contact. If you've been infected, symptoms will usually show up in 1 to 4 weeks.

In females

The most common symptom is a foamy, foul-smelling vaginal discharge that's white or greenish-yellow in colour. The discharge often causes the vulva and vagina to become red and itchy. In some cases, trich extends to the cervix, urethra, and bladder. Some women have a burning sensation when they urinate. For others, intercourse is painful. Some women with trich have no symptoms at all.

In males

The majority of infected men don't have symptoms. For those who do, the tip of their penis may be itchy or irritated, and their urethra may emit a slightly smelly discharge. Untreated, trich can spread through the urethra into the testicles, bladder, and prostate gland.

Getting tested

Only a doctor can diagnose trich. During the examination,
a swab is taken from the vagina if you're female, or the urethra
if you're male. The swab is placed on a slide, which is then put
under a microscope. If there are parasites in the swab, you
have trich.

Unsafe Sex

Another term for unsafe sex is risky sex. If you
have intercourse with someone and you don't use
birth control or protection, you run a very high risk
of starting a pregnancy and catching a sexually
transmitted infection. If you have oral sex or anal
sex without using protection, you only risk catching
an infection. But some of the infections that are very
common are seriously damaging, not only to your
body, but also to your life. For example, teenagers
having unsafe sex with numerous partners are virtually
guaranteed to become infected with chlamydia, which
can lead to sterility if untreated. The statistics are
equally serious for genital warts. And there's still
no cure for HIV, which is spreading among
teenagers at a faster rate than ever.

    Teenagers take the risk of having
unsafe sex for many reasons: they refuse to
believe that pregnancy or disease could happen
to them; they don't recognize their sexuality or
their interest in sex, so when sex "just happens,"
they're not prepared; taking risks is one of
the ways they develop their identities as they
strive to become adults; they're not well-informed
about how easy it is to become pregnant or to catch
an STI; they have low self-esteem and don't care what
happens to them; and more. Having safer sex is also
taking a risk, but the risk is significantly lower because
it's been recognized, thought through, and addressed.

Urethra

This is the tube that carries urine out of the body.

In females ♀

The opening of the urethra is located between the clitoris and the opening to the vagina. Because of its location, the urethra can become irritated during prolonged sexual activity. You'll know this has happened if you feel uncomfortable when you pee after sex (peeing after sex is important to clear away any bacteria that may have been pushed into the urethra during thrusting). This discomfort will disappear in a few hours. If it doesn't, you may have a urinary tract infection and you should see a doctor. **See Cystitis.**

In males ♂

The opening of the urethra is located at the tip of the penis. But urine isn't the only fluid that travels through the urethra. During ejaculation, semen is propelled through the urethra and out of the body. Urine never mixes with semen because a valve closes off the bladder just before ejaculation.

Uterus
↘ womb

Many sex books describe the uterus as an upside-down pear, though unlike a pear, the uterus is hollow and has thick, muscular walls. It's hollow because this is where the foetus develops in a pregnant woman. At the beginning of the pregnancy, the uterus is only about 3 inches long, but it expands as the foetus grows. The walls are muscular in order to push the baby out of the body during birth.

Uterus

The uterus is also where blood collects every month when there's no foetus. Then, at the end of the menstrual cycle, the lining of the uterus breaks down and the blood flows out through the cervix along with tissue and mucus. This is called menstruation. Many people believe that the period pains of menstruation are caused by contractions in the uterus that help push the menstrual flow out of the body.

Q: Will my vagina get loose if I have intercourse too often?

A: The vagina is very elastic, which means it will expand to receive a penis, then shrink back to its original size when the penis is gone. This expand-and-shrink action is the same no matter how many times you have sex.

Q: What's a vaginal orgasm?

A: The inside walls of the vagina can be sensitive, especially in the area of the G-spot. Also, the outside walls of the vagina are surrounded by the legs of the clitoris. With so much to be stimulated, it's understandable that some women climax as a result of friction and pressure in the vagina. Reportedly, vaginal orgasms are less intense than clitoral ones, but more prolonged.

Vagina ♀

↘ box   ↘ hole
↘ crack   ↘ fanny

For many girls who are beginning to learn about their bodies or to have feelings of sexual desire, the vagina can seem distant and unknowable. In fact, it's easy not to know your vagina: you can't see it, no one talks about it, and what comes out of it every month—menstrual flow—is widely considered to be unpleasant, a "curse," and in many cultures, unclean. But not knowing your vagina can be bad for your sex life, and a bad sex life can have a negative impact on life in general.

It makes much more sense to get to know your vagina, and even to like it. It's soft, elastic, warm, muscular, and always moist—actually, the inside of your vagina is a lot like the inside of your mouth. In terms of shape, the vagina is similar to something else—a 7-to-10cm empty tube of toothpaste. Like the empty tube, the walls of the vagina touch each other. When something is inserted, such as a finger or penis or tampon, it expands just enough to hold the object. The vagina's nerve endings are mostly concentrated near the opening, with very few located deeper inside the vagina.

The vagina has 3 primary functions: to funnel menstrual flow out of the body, to receive a penis of any size, and to act as a passageway for a baby. To perform the latter 2 functions, the vagina depends on its elasticity. As the body prepares for penetration by becoming aroused, the vagina lengthens and expands. It does the same thing during childbirth. Arousal also causes the vagina to lubricate, making it a comfortably slippery destination for a thrusting penis, finger, or other object. Lubrication has the second job of creating a welcoming environment for sperm. Penetrating a dry vagina will lead to pain and possibly an infection. When the vagina is first penetrated, the muscle closes tightly around the penis before continuing to expand. During orgasm, the walls contract uncontrollably several times, causing feelings of pleasure.

Vaginal Discharge ♀

The vagina is never dry. To keep itself moist, it continuously produces a small amount of liquid that's referred to as mucus or secretions. This liquid has nowhere to go but out, and when it leaves the vagina, it's called discharge. Healthy discharge is clear or whitish in colour, normal-smelling, and doesn't irritate the skin. Around ovulation you may have more of it, but just for a day or 2 (its consistency will change to slippery or stretchy). Unhealthy discharge is thick or creamy and tends to be an unusual colour such as yellow or pale green, although the discharge from a yeast infection is normally white. It also smells awful and is irritating. This kind of discharge probably means you have a vaginal infection. Or it could be a sign of a sexually transmitted infection, which is more serious. Have a doctor check it out.

Vaginal Infections ♀

Abnormal vaginal discharge usually means you have an infection, which is also called vaginitis.

There are 3 kinds of vaginitis: bacterial vaginosis (BV), trichomoniasis (trich), and candida (yeast infections). Girls frequently get one or more of these infections, sometimes through intercourse, but just as often as a result of stress, an allergy, douching, wearing tight-fitting synthetic clothing, taking antibiotics, or leaving a diaphragm or cervical cap in their vagina for too long. If you think you have a vaginal infection, see a doctor right away for a correct diagnosis and treatment.
See Bacterial Vaginosis, Trichomoniasis, Vaginal Discharge, Yeast Infections.

Q & A ♀

Q: Is yellow discharge in my underwear bad?

A: Healthy discharge turns yellow when it's exposed to air, so don't worry about it unless it smells bad and your vagina is itchy or irritated.

Q: Why do I have lots of discharge once in a while?

A: It's normal to have extra discharge during ovulation, when you're sexually excited, or if you're on the Pill.

Vaginitis in males ♂

Just because guys generally don't show any symptoms of vaginitis, it doesn't mean they're germ-free. If you've had sex with a girl who has a vaginal infection, there's a chance your urethra has been infected with the germs. This means you can pass the germs back to your partner or to other partners. If someone you've slept with tells you she has an infection, make sure you get treated at the same time she does.

Vaginal Odour ♀

It should come as no surprise that the vagina has an odour. After all, it produces a small amount of fluid on a daily basis. This fluid keeps the vagina clean, and its smell is clean too. It's also distinctive. Unfortunately, the "distinctive" part bothers some girls, who worry that their vagina smells bad. A truly bad smell—pungent, yeasty, fishy—is possible, but only if the vagina is infected with one of several infections (particularly BV) or if you don't wash regularly.

Many women proudly refer to their vaginal odour as their "scent." It's one of the ways they identify themselves as sexual beings. They like their scent and feel comfortable with it. When it changes, they can tell whether it's because they have an infection, because they're eating different foods, or because they're having intercourse with a new partner. These women are confident that the way they smell is a sexual stimulant for their partner. It usually is. Many lovers of women—male and female—find a woman's sex smell to be very exciting.

Some women are insecure about their smell and try to hide it by douching, washing with scented soaps, or using vaginal sprays. Ironically, all these activities can throw the pH in the vagina out of balance, resulting in infections that definitely stink. To maintain your natural odour, which in most women is mild to begin with, all you have to do is wash your vulva with warm water and a gentle, unscented soap once a day. Women with a stronger scent may want to wash twice a day. Also, keep your vagina aired out and dry by wearing cotton underwear during the day and sleeping in loose-fitting pyjamas or a nightie at night. See Bacterial Vaginosis (BV), Douching, Vaginal Infections.

Vaginal Orgasm

In recent sexual history there's been a debate over the existence of vaginal orgasms. It began when scientific research uncovered the fact that orgasms could only be achieved through stimulation of the clitoris. If that was true, what about the vaginal orgasms women had been claiming to have for so many years? Were they all faked? Some women insist that vaginal orgasms are possible and report enjoying them. They're described as being less intense than clitoral orgasms, but deeper. Vaginal orgasms may have something to do with the G-spot or with having the clitoris stimulated through the walls of the vagina, either by a penis, fingers, or a dildo.

Vaginismus

Some women can't have intercourse because their vaginal muscles go into painful spasm when penetration is attempted. As a result, the opening to their vagina closes. This condition is called vaginismus, and its roots are usually psychological rather than physical. In other words, most women who suffer from vaginismus are extremely frightened of sex. Some associate sex with pain because of previous negative experiences, others were raped, and still others dread pregnancy or fear their parents' disapproval. Most women can overcome vaginismus with the help of a sex therapist.

When Sex Hurts

If you feel long-term burning, stinging, irritation, or rawness in your vulva, you may have a condition called vulvodynia. The pain can be mild or severe and can often continue over several years. Symptoms often worsen during or after sexual intercourse, sometimes to the point of making penetration impossible. A diagnosis of vulvodynia may take several visits to one or more doctors because the symptoms are similar to those caused by vaginitis, cystitis, and some sexually transmitted infections. While there's no cure for this condition, various treatments can offer relief from the symptoms, which occasionally disappear on their own. Vulvodynia can't be transmitted through sexual contact.

Q & A

Q: If I play with a vibrator and push it into my vagina a bit, does that mean I'm not a virgin?

A: In heterosexual sex, the definition of a virgin is someone who's never had penis-vagina intercourse. In lesbian sex, virginity is lost the first time a woman orgasms with a female partner. Playing with a sex toy has no impact on your status as a virgin.

Venereal Disease
↘VD

This term was used for centuries to refer to diseases you could get by having intercourse with someone who was already infected. Primarily, VD meant syphilis and gonorrhoea. The word venereal comes from the Latin venus veneris, which means sexual love. These days, diseases you can get through sexual contact are called STIs, which stands for sexually transmitted infections. Many people use the term STDs instead (sexually transmitted diseases), but this is considered inaccurate as the majority of STIs start out as infections, not diseases, and many can be cured before damage is done to the body. See Sexually Transmitted Infections.

Vibrators

These popular, battery-operated sex toys are usually used to stimulate the clitoris, though some men enjoy the way they feel against their erect penis. Because it's so easy for women to orgasm using a vibrator (by holding it against the vaginal lips) it's tempting to use one all the time. The trouble with relying on this handy device is that it rules out masturbating, which is one of the best ways to learn about your body. As you become skilful at masturbating, you'll learn what turns you on and what doesn't, and you can communicate those things to your partner and improve your sexual relationship.

People who use vibrators generally have their own, but if you're sharing, make sure you disinfect it before giving it to your partner. You can do this by wiping it with a bleach-water solution (1 part bleach to 10 parts water), then rinsing with water. Or you can use the vibrator with a condom, but remember to put on a new condom before passing it to your partner. Vibrators can be purchased in sex shops, but to enter a licensed sex shop you must be 18 or over. See Dildos.

Virginity

Virginity describes that time in a person's life after they become sexually mature and before they've had sexual intercourse for the first time, or in the case of lesbians and gay men, before they've been brought to orgasm by a partner for the first time. Traditionally the word virginity described far more than the state of someone's sexual experience. People who were virgins were thought to still have their innocence and purity intact. To many people, this mostly related to girls, who were expected to be pure and innocent. Though technically guys can be virgins too, for most of human history no value has been attached to their virginity. On the contrary, young males have been expected to confirm their masculine identity by "sowing their seed." In some parts of the world, female virginity is still closely guarded by family and law.

Ironically, there's less emphasis these days on virginity and more emphasis on losing it. It's not uncommon for both girls and guys to be harassed by their peers if they've reached a certain age and still haven't had sex (the age differs from group to group). Even if the jokes were begun in fun, they wear pretty thin after a while. Some girls and guys end up having first sex just to get it over with. Not surprisingly, the pressure of having sex under these conditions frequently spoils any possible pleasure. It's also dangerous because the decision is often made on the spur of the moment and people tend not to have protection handy. See Double Standard.

Most of the time, the best way to lose your virginity is to plan it. It follows that good first sex has a higher chance of leading to further experiences of good sex and ultimately to a good sex life. On the contrary, first sex that's bad can turn you off for a long time or decimate your confidence. You're more likely to have a positive first experience if you trust and really like or love your partner, and the feelings are mutual. And don't forget to use protection! Sex when you lose your virginity can lead to pregnancy or infection just as easily as sex at any other time. See Birth Control, Protection, Safer Sex.

Lots of girls have "wet dreams," though no one calls them that. Actually, no name has been given to the phenomenon of girls having dreams that are so sexually or otherwise exciting that their vagina becomes lubricated and they orgasm. This could be because our society has a history of not recognizing female desire. Or, the explanation could be much simpler: if there are no sheets to change, there's nothing to talk about. As with boys, sometimes the dreams are remembered, sometimes they're not.

Vulva

↘pussy ↘snatch
↘cunt ↘muff
↘bush ↘twat

Long ago, the gateway to the female reproductive system was named "vulva" after one of Scandinavia's most ancient and powerful goddesses.

The vulva includes the labia majora, the labia minora (both of which are also called the lips), the opening to the vagina, the opening to the urethra, the clitoris, and the hood. Girls should be familiar with this important part of the female body. Self-knowledge always comes in handy when decisions have to be made about sex. See Clitoris, Labia Majora, Labia Minora, Mons, Vagina.

To all female readers: if you have a few moments, take a mirror and check out your vulva.

Wet Dreams

Beginning in puberty, boys frequently wake up at night to find their pyjamas or blankets are wet with a bit of semen. Without knowing it, they've ejaculated, probably because they've dreamed about something sexy or adventurous. Sometimes they remember the dream, sometimes they don't. Very often a boy's first ejaculation occurs at night. If he hasn't been warned that this will happen, it can be confusing. Wet dreams taper off over time and are rarely experienced by adults.

Q: Can I get pregnant if my boyfriend puts his penis in my vagina just for a second?

A: It only takes a second for sperm in pre-ejaculate to swim up your vagina. Even if his penis is in and out in a flash, it's still called intercourse, and unprotected intercourse can lead to pregnancy. It can also lead to sexually transmitted infections. Make sure he wears a condom every time.

Guys:
Even if you pull out of your partner's vagina before coming, you can still catch sexually transmitted infections, and you can still pass them on. Keep everyone happy by wearing a condom.

Wishful Thinking

You don't have to believe in magic to be guilty of wishful thinking. If you're a guy, this is when you feel certain you won't get your girlfriend pregnant even though you're having unprotected sex. If you're a girl, it's fooling yourself into believing that pregnancy is something that happens to other people, not you. Regardless of your sex, if you're having intercourse and you're not using birth control, you have a 25% chance of starting a pregnancy this month. People also engage in wishful thinking when it comes to sexually transmitted infections. Here'a a typical example: "I only sleep with really nice-looking people who would never give me an infection."

Withdrawal

↘ coitus interruptus
↘ pulling out

There are 3 reasons why withdrawal shouldn't be relied on to prevent pregnancies. First, it involves the guy pulling his penis out of his partner's vagina before he ejaculates…and what if he doesn't pull out in time? Guys will admit that it's very tempting to stay in, with the result that sperm may achieve their biological destiny: to fertilize an egg. Also, guys don't always know when they're going to ejaculate.

Second, even if he pulls out before ejaculating, it may be too late. Pre-ejaculate may have already leaked into the vagina, and pre-ejaculate contains sperm. Finally, this kind of "birth control" leaves the female partner without any control at all. Since she's the one risking pregnancy, she should play at least an equal part in making sure the birth control is effective. See Birth Control, Pre-ejaculate.

Womb

This is the common word for uterus. In a pregnant woman, it's the place where the baby develops until it's born. The word "womb" also refers to any place that's warm and safe and nourishing. See Uterus.

Yeast Infections

↘candida ↘thrush

Candida is a fungus that normally exists in healthy amounts in the mouth and intestines. In women, it's also found in the vagina. Sometimes, the candida in the vagina multiplies out of control. The first sign that this has happened is mild itching in the vaginal area. Women who've never had a yeast infection might scratch themselves a couple of times and think nothing of it. Women who've had one, or maybe several, recognize the itch and head straight to the chemists for an anti-fungal medication, or they hurry to the kitchen to prepare a home remedy. They want to avoid what frequently comes next, which is an itching that's so intense, it's actually painful.

When candida overgrows in the vagina, there's a reason for it. It can happen if you're on antibiotics, very occasionally if you're on the Pill, or if you're feeling unusually tired or stressed. Many women find that the yeast infection is aggravated by wearing nylon underwear, tights, or tight, synthetic clothing.

There is no evidence that yeast infections in women are acquired through sex. Occasionally guys may develop a rash on their penis from a yeast infection caught from their girlfriend. Even for women with frequent vaginal yeast infections, the male partner should only seek treatment if he himself has symptoms.

Q & A ♀

Q: If I have a yeast infection, can I have sex with my boyfriend if he wears a condom?

A: If you're trying to clear up your infection by using a cream or vaginal suppository, his condom will be destroyed by agents in the medication. As a result, you could get pregnant or catch a sexually transmitted infection. At the same time, he could get your yeast infection. Anyway, it's often painful to have sex if you have a yeast infection. It's a good idea to wait until the infection is gone.

Q: Do I have to treat a yeast infection or will it go away on its own?

A: Sometimes yeast infections show up, are very mild, and go away after a few days. This usually happens during menstruation. If the infection comes back after your period is over, or if it lasts for more than a few days, it's best to treat it and avoid the extreme itchiness that's sure to come.

In ♀ females

Besides experiencing mild or severe itching in and around your vagina, your discharge will probably be thick, white, and lumpy, a bit like cottage cheese. Some women say it's odourless; others describe a yeasty smell. Urination can be painful. Most women have had a yeast infection at one time or another, and some women get them frequently.

In males ♂

Men often don't have symptoms, especially if they're circumcised (symptoms are more likely to develop on uncircumcised penises). Men with symptoms will see a redness at the tip of their penis and the head may be covered with small red dots. Sometimes the head has a scalded look and is covered by a film that can be wiped off. The tip may be itchy or sore, and the testicles may also itch.

Getting tested

It's important to have a doctor confirm that what you have is a yeast infection and not something else. The diagnosis is usually made by observing the symptoms. If your problem turns out to be something else, at least you'll get treated for it. If in fact you have a yeast infection, the diagnosis will help you recognize the symptoms should you become infected again.

Treatment

Creams and vaginal suppositories designed to fight yeast infections can be purchased over the counter at most chemists. Before making your purchase, it's important to be certain that you actually have a yeast infection. If none of these remedies work, ask your doctor to prescribe a medication. Some women, fed up with the cost of medications and concerned about drug use, prefer to treat their yeast infections with supplements and home remedies that make use of yogurt, garlic, or herbs. To find out more about home remedies, see a naturopathic doctor. Some people advise changing your underwear a couple of times a day while you're fighting the infection, as candida can live on cotton.

Prevention

Yeast infections can often be prevented. Here are some tips: wear cotton undies during the day and no undies at night while you sleep; don't wear tights or close-fitting trousers; don't bring chemicals into contact with your vulva (douches, scented soaps, scented products of any kind); dry your vulva very well after having a bath or shower; wipe from front to back after going to the toilet; and if you're on antibiotics, think about taking acidophilus supplements (acidophilus can be purchased at most health food stores and some pharmacies). Also, don't have oral sex or intercourse with someone who's infected. If you're infected, keep it to yourself by avoiding sexual activities until your infection is cleared up.

Zzz

A deep and contented sleep, which is often what comes next after having good sex with someone you love.

RESOURCES

In the U.K., calls from landlines to 0845 numbers are charged at local rate and calls to 0800 numbers are free.

General

Brook Advisory Centre
Free, confidential advice on sex and contraception.
Help line: 0800 0185 023 (Mon—Fri 9am—5pm)
www.brook.org.uk

Family Planning Association
Provides information on all aspects of sexual health and reproductive rights and choices (including contraception).
Help line: 0845 310 1334 (Mon—Fri 9am—7pm)
www.fpa.org.uk

Get Connected
Support for young people on any issue and free connection to services which can help.
Help line: 0808 808 4994 (Mon—Sun 1—11pm, calls free from most mobiles).
www.getconnected.org.uk

Marie Stopes International
Sexual and reproductive health information and services.
Help line: 0800 716 390 (Mon—Fri 7am—10pm, Sat-Sun 8am—6pm)
www.mariestopes.org.uk

NHS Direct
24-hour confidential help line answering all questions about health concerns.
Help line: 0845 46 47 (Mon—Sun, 24 hours)
www.nhsdirect.nhs.uk

Sexwise
Confidential help for teenagers on anything to do with sex, relationships and contraception.
Help line: 0800 28 29 30
(Mon—Sun 7am—midnight)
www.ruthinking.co.uk

Abortion and Pregnancy

British Pregnancy Advisory Service
Confidential info, counselling and treatment on contraception, pregnancy and abortion. Phone for an appointment to talk over your options.
Action line: 08457 30 40 30 (Mon—Fri 8am—9pm, Sat 8am—6pm, Sun 9.30am—2.30pm)
www.bpas.org.uk

National Abortion Campaign
Campaigning for women's right to decide what they do with their bodies and for equal access to safe, free abortion on request.
Help line: 020 7923 4976 (Mon and Thurs, 9am—4.30pm)
http://nac.gn.apc.org

HIV and AIDS

National AIDS helpline
Help line: 0800 567 123 (Mon—Sun, 24 hours)

Terrence Higgins Trust
Offers support if you are living with HIV, know someone who is, or if you might be at risk of HIV.
Help line: 0845 122 1200 (Mon—Fri 10am—10pm, Sat—Sun 12—6pm) www.tht.org.uk

The Law

Children's Legal Centre
Confidential legal information and advice on all aspects of the law affecting young people.
Help line: 01206 873 820 (Mon—Fri 10am—12.30pm 2—4.30 pm)
www.childrenslegalcentre.com

Lesbian/Bi/Gay

London Lesbian and Gay Switchboard
For info on lesbian, gay, bisexual and transgender issues.
Help line: 020 7837 7324 (Mon—Sun, aims at 24-hour service)
www.queery.org.uk

RESOURCES

Stonewall
Provides info on legal and social issues for lesbians, gays and bisexuals.
Help line: 020 7881 9440 (Mon—Fri 9.30am—5.30pm)
www.stonewall.org.uk

STIs

When you need advice about STIs, there are several places you can go to for help:
- NHS genitourinary medicine clinic (also known as GU, GUM, STD or special clinics)
- your G.P. or practice nurse
- sexual health clinic
- family planning clinic
- young people's clinic

You can find details of local clinics in the telephone directory. All advice, information and tests are free and confidential. Nothing will be done without your permission. Alternatively, try the help lines and websites in the "General" section above.

Rape and Abusive Relationships

Drug Rape Trust
Offers advice and support to anyone who thinks they might have been drugged and attacked. (Service suspended at time of going to press.)
01702 317695
www.drugrapetrust.org

NSPCC (National Society for Prevention of Cruelty to Children)
Professional counselling, advice and info for anyone concerned about a young person at risk of ill treatment or abuse.
Help line: 0800 800 5000 (Mon—Sun, 24 hours)
www.nspcc.org.uk

Rape Crisis Federation (Wales and England)
Gives advice and support around the issues of rape and sexual abuse or assault. Refers you to your nearest Rape Crisis Centre.
Help line: 0115 900 3560 (Mon—Fri 9am—5pm)
www.rapecrisis.co.uk

RASASC (Rape and Sexual Abuse Support Centre)
Confidential, non-judgemental help for female victims of rape or sexual abuse.
Help line: 020 8683 3300 (Mon—Fri 12—2.30pm 7—9.30pm, Sat—Sun 2.30—5pm
www.rasasc.org.uk

Talking to someone

Careline
Crisis counselling by phone for all age groups on any issue.
Help line: 020 8514 1177 (Mon—Fri 10am—4pm 7—10pm)

Childline
Free, 24-hour helpline for young people to talk to a trained counsellor about anything that's bothering them.
0800 1111 (Mon—Sun, 24 hours)
www.childline.org.uk

Eire

For anyone in the Republic of Ireland who needs more information on sexual and related issues, the IFPA is a good place to start. If they can't help you directly, they'll be able to refer you to someone who can:

Irish Family Planning Association
Answers any questions on sexual and reproductive rights and health.
National Pregnancy Help Line: 1850 49 50 51
www.ifpa.ie

Index